Mini-Aquariums

David E. Boruchowitz

Mini-Aquariums
A Guide to Successful Nano Aquariums

Project Team
Editor: Craig Sernotti
Copy Editor: Neal Pronek
Indexer: Joann Woy
Design: Mary Ann Kahn
Cover Design: Mary Ann Kahn

TFH Publications
President/CEO: Glen S. Axelrod
Executive Vice President: Mark E. Johnson
Publisher: Christopher T. Reggio
Production Manager: Kathy Bontz

T.F.H. Publications, Inc.
One TFH Plaza
Third and Union Avenues
Neptune City, NJ 07753

Printed and bound in China
08 09 10 11 12   1 3 5 7 9 8 6 4 2

Library of Congress Cataloging-in-Publication Data
Boruchowitz, David E.
  Mini aquariums / David E. Boruchowitz.
      p. cm.
  Includes index.
  ISBN 978-0-7938-0573-0 (alk. paper)
  1. Aquariums 2. Aquarium fishes. I. Title.
  SF457.3.B684 2008
  639.34—dc22
                    2007030146

This book has been published with the intent to provide accurate and authoritative information in regard to the subject matter within. While every reasonable precaution has been taken in preparation of this book, the author and publisher expressly disclaim responsibility for any errors, omissions, or adverse effects arising from the use or application of the information contained herein. The techniques and suggestions are used at the reader's discretion and are not to be considered a substitute for veterinary care. If you suspect a medical problem consult your veterinarian.

The Leader In Responsible Animal Care For Over 50 Years!®
www.tfh.com

Contents

Preface

I must confess up front. I am a cichlidiot who thinks of a 55-gallon (200-liter) tank as midsize and dreams of flooding most of the house in order to finally get a decent-sized aquarium. But I'm also very excited about miniature aquaria, or nano tanks. Oh, I still have tanks big enough for my grandchildren to swim in, and I've still got plans for that ultimate built-in "lake." But I also have some small—no, mini—tanks, and I plan on setting up more. I'd like to introduce this book with an example from the 5-gallon (20-liter) hex setup on my desk as I write this.

I'd been eyeing nano setups with considerable curiosity for a while when a few years ago I got some fish on a whim—*Boraras maculatus,* one of the smallest of the rasboras. Those little jewels fully opened my eyes to the otherwise unattainable aquaristic experiences that tiny tanks can provide. They made a wonderful school in a 20-gallon (80-liter) tank, but it wasn't until I moved them into a nano of their own that I could truly appreciate their beauty and grace. In the larger aquarium they were basically a mass of moving red dots. At any given time they took up a very small percentage of the visual field, and they tended to run and hide whenever one of their small-but-not-tiny tankmates came near. When I placed them in a 3-gallon (11-liter) tank by themselves, they relaxed a bit and spread out, and since they were the only fish in there, I often got up close to watch them. I even started putting on my reading glasses to view them clearly with my nose against the glass.

I enjoyed this aquarium so much I decided to move further into the nano experience with a 5-gallon (20-liter) community setup. Of course I included a dozen of the rasboras. I chose as tankmates some of those tiny sparkling gouramis *Trichopsis pumila.* You may

Trichopsis pumila

know of the fish. In the literature they're described as so peaceful that in a community tank they may not get anything to eat. Well, don't believe it. They're nasty brutes. They just aren't stupid brutes. Their maximum size is supposed to be 4.0 centimeters, which is about 1.6 inches. Most of the ones I've seen fall rather short of that, but in any case 1½ inches isn't very large. These are fish that know their limits; they won't take on larger fish, but put them in a tank of their own, and you'll immediately see some definite bickering. Add some *B. maculatus*, and you'll see the nasty brutes.

No, they're not Jekyll/Hyde fish, they just demonstrate that peaceful and aggressive behaviors are often relative. A small cichlid that takes forever to approach, haltingly darting forward and then backward when you offer it food by hand, will not hesitate an instant to latch its jaws onto your hand if that hand comes too close to eggs or fry. And a tiny gourami that feeds timidly in a standard community tank will, once it discovers it is the biggest fish in the aquarium, assert itself vigorously. The *Trichopsis* never injured the rasboras, but they aggressively kept them away, especially at feeding time.

Eventually I moved the gouramis to the tank housing my *Xiphophorus montezumae* colony, where they quickly resumed the bashful behavior they are known for. In their stead I added a small colony of cherry red shrimp. It took the rasboras a few days to be certain they were the only fish in the tank, and after I added the shrimp, they also required a few days before they felt safe enough to come out of hiding. The shrimp are a bit larger than the fish, and the two species now ignore each other completely. The shrimp are busy all the time. They reside down in a clump of Java moss, but they swim around the tank and police the glass sides and gravel for snippets of algae or fish food. Recently I've started to see a lot of juveniles, which means that at least some of the baby shrimp are avoiding predation. I figure they stay in the moss until they are large enough not to be eaten. The rasboras are visible most of the time, usually broken up into several small loose schools. They also have responded to their elevation in position. One dominant individual now bosses all the others around, and an obvious pecking order has replaced the uniformly timid schooling they manifested in the presence of other fish.

Both of these animals would be all but invisible in a regular community tank with larger fishes. Not only would they be hiding most of the time, they would be hard to see only a few feet away. There would be little chance of the shrimp reproducing successfully, and, in fact, even the adult rasboras and shrimp might be in danger. Instead, they are confident extroverts in the desktop tank, which is only inches from me as I work. Dozens of times during the day I glance over and watch for a few seconds, catching all of their behaviors and enjoying their colors and grace. This is what a nano tank is all about!

You see, the nano experience isn't about keeping fish in little tanks. No, it's about keeping nano setups, nano displays. What's the difference? Well, you can put a couple of comet goldfish in a bowl or four platies in a 5-gallon (20-liter) tank, but all you get from that is some crowded, unhappy fish. On the other hand, substitute a school of *B. maculatus* and you have a fascinating aquarium in which the fish exhibit a full range of natural behaviors. The nano setup takes a magnifying glass to a regular aquatic system. And it magnifies the enjoyment we can get from the smallest aquatic creatures while beautifying our homes and offices.

Now, if only I'd started keeping nano tanks before I needed reading glasses to see the fish clearly!

The Evolution of the Nano Concept

Chapter **1**

Until the middle of the last century a 20-gallon (75-liter) aquarium was about the largest commonly found in the hobby, and 2 ½-, 5-, and 10-gallon (10-, 20-, and 40-liter) tanks were prevalent. When this changed, several other changes also occurred in the hobby to take attention away from small aquaria other than as breeding, quarantine, or temporary holding tanks.

Size Limits

Back then, large fish could not normally be kept at all, and even many small- to mid-size species were cramped in these little aquaria. In addition, tanks were easily overcrowded, since a hobbyist wishing to keep even a minimal mixture of species quickly wound up with more fish flesh than a small tank could properly handle.

The small spaces also fostered aggression, and fish, like some cichlids, got undeservedly bad reputations. If an even mildly territorial animal has a minimum acceptable territorial area that is the same or greater than the area of the aquarium floor, it will kill every other fish in the aquarium. For example, *"Cichlasoma" octofasciatum* was called the Jack Dempsey after the famous prizefighter. In a 100-gallon (400-liter) community of Central American cichlids this fish is not markedly more aggressive than most of its tankmates—and in fact is less aggressive than some others—but in a 10- or 15-gallon (40- or 60-liter) community tank of livebearers and tetras it is a vicious killer. And heaven help the other fish if two Dempseys paired up and spawned!

As larger aquaria became more commonly available, larger fish became more popular. Simultaneously, the cichlid craze of the last 40 years began as all-glass tanks began to make large tanks economically viable. The aquarium size explosion was underway!

Equipment Proliferation

The technological advancements of the last half of the twentieth century affected the aquarium hobby in many ways. For example, space age materials made aquaria lighter, stronger, and more reliable, and this made large aquaria a more popular option. Flexibility in design led to truly ornamental fish tanks. Developments in lighting technology permitted an explosion in the fields of freshwater planted tanks and marine invertebrate reef tanks. Improvements in global travel and exploration led to a massive increase in the species available in the hobby—the explosive growth of specialties like African Rift Lake cichlids and South American loricariid catfish are but two examples.

During this period in which aquarium science and aquarium technology rose to new levels, the 4-foot, 55-gallon (120-cm, 200-liter) aquarium became very popular, and many hobbyists even had 100-gallon (400-liter) or larger tanks in their homes. While all this was happening, many new items of aquarium equipment entered the market, and they were manufactured for the larger tanks of the day. As a consequence, a line was drawn between the old aquaria and "modern" setups: between small tanks and measly air-driven filters and large tanks with power filters, between mini tanks with incandescent fixtures and more substantial tanks with high-tech lighting. All of this served to push small tanks further out of the mainstream hobby.

Small Tanks in the Modern Hobby

Throughout this time and up through today, small tanks remained on the scene in three principal uses, all supplementary to the main hobby: goldfish bowls, beginner tanks, and killifish breeding tanks.

The goldfish bowl and the small tank have always been favored by beginners. The cost outlay is small, the impact on the home's decor is minimal, and it seems as if

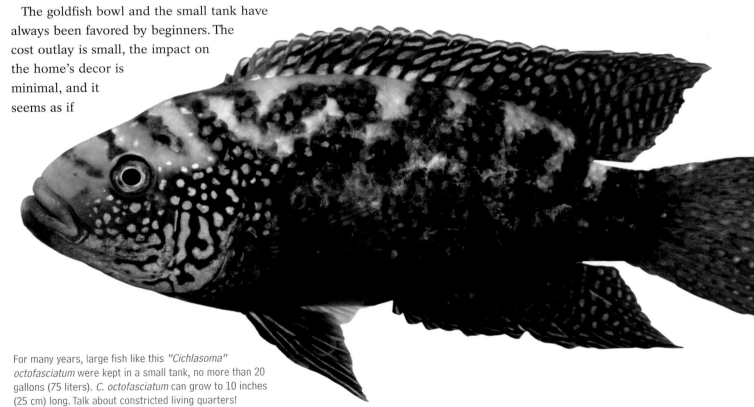

For many years, large fish like this "Cichlasoma" octofasciatum were kept in a small tank, no more than 20 gallons (75 liters). C. octofasciatum can grow to 10 inches (25 cm) long. Talk about constricted living quarters!

11

maintenance will be quick and easy. Unfortunately, both a goldfish bowl and a small tank for a beginner are extremely bad ideas.

Goldfish Bowls

Goldfish are heavy-bodied, heavy-feeding fish that need heavy filtration and should have between 10 and 20 gallons (40 and 80 liters) of water per fish. They are, however, very hardy fish that can survive gruesome conditions. This, plus the ease with which they can be replaced when they die, keeps them popular as bowl fish. In reality, though, thousands perish in bowls, many languish in bowls, and none thrive in bowls. Goldfish bowls are very serviceable things with many uses—they just make lousy homes for goldfish.

Goldfish are under no circumstances appropriate candidates for a nano aquarium. They need large tanks and simply cannot do well when deprived of the room they need. Keeping a goldfish in a bowl or small tank is the equivalent of locking a Saint Bernard in a closet. We will not discuss goldfish further in regard to nano aquaria. (Goldfish, however, can be kept in a nano pond. See Chapter 10.)

Goldfish require tanks much larger than those that are discussed in this book; they should not be part of your nano tank setup.

Beginner Tanks

The misguided recommendation of a small beginner tank assumes that a limited volume of water is easier to keep clean in the same way that it takes less time to wash a subcompact car than a stretch limousine. Unfortunately, with aquaria the opposite is true—it is much easier to maintain a stable water chemistry in a large tank than in a small one, and chemical instability is the leading cause of aquarium fish deaths. Since fish deaths are the leading cause of beginners' giving up the hobby in frustration, recommending a small tank to a new aquarist is extremely bad advice.

This also holds for nano aquaria. It is certainly possible for someone to maintain a successful nano aquarium as a first tank, but it is hundreds of times more likely for a new hobbyist to succeed with a larger tank. This book is therefore written for aquarists with some experience in the hobby—people who understand cycling and filtration and basic fish husbandry. If you are just starting out, I encourage you to wait for your nano setup, but if you really want to start with it, then this book will still be very useful. Only please do yourself and your fish a favor and also read extensively about basic aquarium setup and maintenance.

Killie Tanks

Killifish represent a major specialty in the hobby, but their keeping is outside the mainstream. There are many reasons for the lack of interest on the part of the average aquarist, despite the fact that killies are extremely beautiful and interesting fish; these reasons include the necessity of keeping most killie species in breeding groups in small individual aquaria. Among hobbyists today, killifish breeders are the ones most likely to use small aquaria, and many of them have fishrooms full of tanks of 5 gallons (20 liters) or less.

Other than in the three foregoing uses, small tanks were until quite recently relegated to the status of temporary vessels—quarantine tanks, hospital tanks, and holding tanks. Some aquarists would use them for fry, but that is also a temporary use.

A Spotlight of Their Own

In the last decade or so, mini aquaria have come into a light of their own, and the modern nano tank concept has emerged. The development of the term "nano aquarium" is in itself instructive. When knowledge and technology advanced to the point that maintaining an aquarium focused on sessile marine invertebrates—principally corals—became possible for the home aquarist, the tanks were called "mini-reefs," indicating that they represented a spotlight on natural tropical coral reefs. Although

A killifish, *Aphyosemion striatum*. Although beautiful and of the perfect size for a nano setup, most killifish are not sold at pet or aquarium stores. They have to be purchased directly from killie dealers and/or breeders.

"mini" in terms of an oceanic reef, many of these tanks were 100 gallons (400 liters) or even much more.

When knowledge and technology progressed to the point that smaller reef aquaria were possible, they were called "nano" reefs, and, by analogy, the smallest desktop reefs were called "pico." These definitions, of course, are not set in stone, and over time things have simplified. For the purposes of this book, we will use the term "nano aquarium" to refer to systems satisfying two requirements: being generally of small size, in most cases 10 gallons (40 liters) or less, and having a microscopic focus. Of these, the latter is more important, since it is the tight focus that distinguishes a nano tank from a regular setup of the same size. It stands to reason, then, that fairly large setups can have a nano focus as well, and we will investigate this extreme in Chapter 11.

Metric Prefixes

The technical prefixes co-opted by aquarists come from the series that includes:

Prefix	Meaning	Decimal	Exponent
Milli-	thousandth	.001	10-3
Micro-	millionth	.000001	10-6
Nano-	billionth	.000000001	10-9
Pico-	trillionth	.000000000001	10-12

In math and science, there is no definition for "mini," but by analogy it falls into the "micro" slot here. Obviously, when applied to aquaria the prefixes are being used figuratively, since if a one-gallon tank were truly "nano," a regular aquarium would be 1,000,000,000 gallons!

Without trying to understand all the causal relationships among them (and these factors certainly feed into each other), we can look at five major factors involved in the development of the nano concept.

Decorative Aquaria

Although aquaria have long been used in interior decoration, in recent years the popularity of this practice has reached new heights. Aquarium maintenance companies permit people with no experience or interest in setting up and maintaining an aquarium to enjoy the beauty of a fish or a reef tank in their homes and offices. Spectacular display aquaria are also found in public places, like airport terminals and hotel lobbies.

At the same time, the popularity of desktop aquaria has risen. Style and ornament are crucial to these as well, but the built-in requirement that the setup be unobtrusive on a desk limits its size to a few gallons. When the focus of a small aquarium is decorative, it requires much more than simply a nice-looking system. Large display tanks often get much of their appeal from their size—the sheer volume is impressive, as are the large fish that can be kept in them. A small tank that is simply a scaled-down version of a big tank is a ho-hum disappointment. Artistically, the desktop aquarium should be as impressive as a wall-sized display; by focusing on the tiny, on things that would go unnoticed in a large aquarium, it can be.

Proliferation of Forms

Modern fabrication materials and technologies have given rise to an enormous variety of aquaria, including those of desktop size. Tanks can be made in just about any shape, and many desktop aquaria are round, hexagonal, bow-front, or some other non-traditional shape. There are tanks connected with tubular swim-throughs, tanks built into furniture, aquarium room dividers, coffee table aquaria, and tanks integrated into plumbing fixtures and old computer monitors.

An enclosed 6-ounce (170-gram) pico aquarium.

Desktop aquaria can now come in shapes and sizes once considered impossible or unobtainable.

Miniaturized Equipment

As desktop tanks became more popular, aquarists became more frustrated. An unheated, unlit, and unfiltered aquarium was not an option for these serious hobbyists, but it was very difficult to find equipment small enough for these setups. This new market did not go unnoticed by aquarium equipment manufacturers, and an ever-increasing number of heating, cooling, lighting, and filtration units are available. You can now get reef-caliber nano lights and moon lights, nano power filters, tiny heaters, miniature skimmers, etc., with more products coming onto the market all the time.

This has been important in the proliferation of nano tanks, since plunking a regular sponge filter and heater into many of them would just about fill the aquarium. Even the smallest regular power filter would turn a tiny tank into a whirlpool bath, and even the lowest-wattage heater would alternately cook and chill such a small volume of water. In addition, an airline looks like an intrusion in the small space, and all but the weakest flow rates will roil the water. Miniaturized power filters solve these problems, providing the same level of filtration aquarists are used to, only scaled down for these desktop systems. Miniaturized heaters enable aquarists to properly heat a nano aquarium.

A prominent trend is toward all-in-one units in which lighting and/or filtration are integral with the aquarium itself. Various designs exist, including systems that incorporate the filtration into the hood, units that have all the equipment in a space at the back of the aquarium, and tiny high-tech lights mounted on stalks above the tank rim.

Availability of Fishes

No matter what type of fish you are interested in, the supply today is the greatest and most varied it has ever been, and this holds true in the field of nano fish as well. Perhaps the most exciting is the flood of new species of small cyprinids (primarily danios and rasboras) coming in from Southeast Asia. Many of these are newly discovered species, while others are animals already known to science, but coming into the hobby from new markets, like Burma (also known as Myanmar) and Vietnam. Although a bit more specialized, the ranks of the so-called "wild bettas" are increasing all the time with more species being discovered and imported, often by aquarists who go to the Far East to collect them.

Danio choprai (left) and *Trigonostigma hengeli* (right). Just two of the newest fish that have been discovered and introduced to the aquarium hobby.

A large group of these new species are congeners (in the same genus) of long-time favorites. For example, the ever-popular rasbora *Trigonostigma heteromorpha* has been joined by *T. espei* and *T. hengeli*. The staple danios (recently moved from the genus *Brachydanio* into *Danio*) now share tank space at retailers' shops with *D. kyathit*, *D. choprai*, and others. Even the long-monotypic white cloud *Tanichthys albonubes* now has a congener, *T. micagemmae*, a recent import from Vietnam.

In addition, fish that were extremely rare (and very expensive) in the hobby, like the chocolate gourami, *Sphaerichthys osphromenoides*, are now imported with much more frequency, and they do not command such high prices any more. All of these increased sources of fish serve the nano side of the hobby as well as the others.

A Focus on Invertebrates

Long a favorite of marine aquarists, invertebrates have finally come into their own in the freshwater hobby as well. Tiny freshwater shrimp are especially popular, both for their algae-eating proclivities and for their variety of color morphs. They first became well known because they will eat algae in planted tanks in which algae-eating fish are often unwelcome because of their size or boisterousness. Many aquarists became enamored of the wee crustaceans, which get quickly lost—or eaten—in a typical community fish tank. The nano tank was an obvious solution to the problem of displaying and maintaining these shrimps.

The Nano Concept

Any aquarium setup is a microcosm based to various degrees on the macrocosm of fish in their natural habitats. Biotope systems are more closely and purposely based, but even a garish setup with neon-colored plastic plants, bubble-up ornaments, and capriciously chosen species does represent a microscopic view of the natural world—its purpose is to showcase some aspect of Nature in the confines of the glass box.

Within this framework, a nano tank tightens the view considerably in order to showcase the concept of an aquarium at the micro level. It's this inward focus that makes the nano tank different from—and much more than—just a small tank. It isn't simply Nature being focused, it's the very concept of focusing on Nature that is highlighted. The balance and dynamics of the natural aquatic world are magnified and displayed in the nano aquarium.

Spectacle in Miniature

I've already mentioned that nano tanks can be as impressive in their smallness as giant display tanks are in their grandeur. This is really the other side of this focus-within-a-focus concept. A huge tank says, in effect: *Look! This is what it looks like in an ocean, lake, or river.* A nano tank says: *Look closely! There is plenty happening at the micro level in an ocean, lake, or river.*

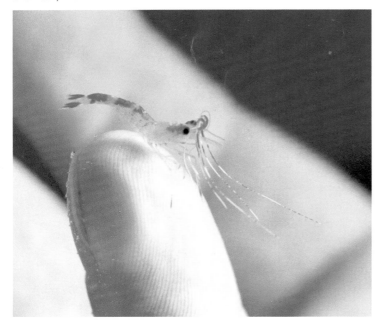

Lysmata amboinensis, a saltwater shrimp. A nano setup forces you to stop and admire the beauty in smallness, and small beauties.

A nano setup is also a great place for appropriately sized specimens that are shy, nocturnal, or otherwise rarely out and about. A small tank gives them fewer places to hide, and kept on a desk, viewed all the time, they are more likely to be spotted during their brief appearances. Even with more extrovert species, you will find that by being able to glance at them throughout the day you will gain a new understanding of and appreciation for their behaviors.

A Bonsai Philosophy

The oriental art form known as *bonsai* has a 2,000-year head start and involves techniques unrelated to keeping aquaria, but the philosophy behind it is quite similar to that of nano aquaria. A sugar maple seedling 12 inches (30 cm) high might have a half dozen full-sized leaves on a single barely woody stem. Stick it in a pot and you do not have an artistic or decorative houseplant; you have instead a plant that looks pot-bound, a baby tree trying to masquerade as something else. On the other hand, a 75-year-old bonsai maple of the same height might have several gnarled branches sporting a full canopy of miniature leaves. It looks like a wizened tree on some windswept hill, only shrunk down to reside happily in a small ceramic dish. It evokes all the grace and beauty of a prized tree specimen, only symmetrically shrunk to fit on a tabletop. Now, with aquaria we are not interested in stunting or dwarfing organisms, but the philosophy of recreating in miniature some larger aspect of Nature is the same.

Adopting a bonsai philosophy will help you unlock the joy of nano aquaria.

A Nano Overview

Within our definition of a nano aquarium as one small in size with a micro focus there are three basic types of setups, depending on how the nano concept is implemented.

Specimen Display

One possible focus is on a species that for whatever reason would be unremarkable in a regular community. Placed by themselves, one or more individuals can be observed closely. A nano breeding tank is not out of the question, as any species that does not prey heavily on its eggs or fry will establish a breeding colony in an aquarium without competition from other fish. Where size is compatible, a nano system is a great way to display a single specimen of a species that cannot be kept with other fish—which can be for a variety of reasons.

Community Display

The most common type of nano aquarium, the community display, does on a miniature level what the regular community tank does. The smallest of decorations, plants, and animals are combined to present a balanced, spacious display. It is important to keep to scale; the nano system is not just small, it's miniaturized.

Biotope Display

The increasingly popular biotope aquarium also has its nano application. In a biotope setup the plants, animals, even substrate are chosen to match a specific natural habitat, or biotope. A nano biotope will, of course, have a very tight focus, which can manifest itself as either a spotlight on a specific microhabitat or a focus on the smallest inhabitants of a particular biotope.

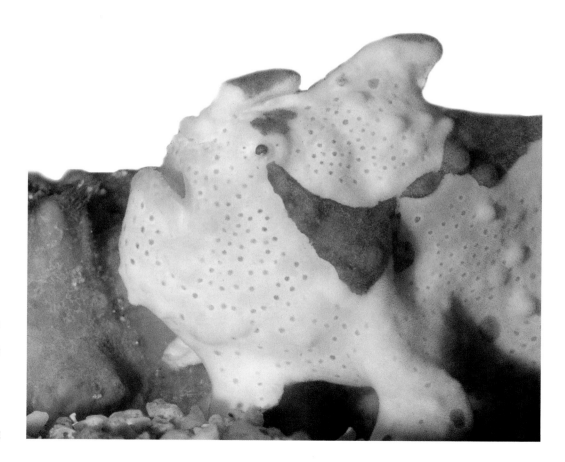

Certain species are just too voracious or volatile to be kept in a community tank. Such specimens, like this warty frogfish *Antennarius maculatus* (a saltwater fish), can and should be kept in a single specimen tank. The reason being because a frogfish has the proverbial gaping maw: it can swallow fish almost as long as it is!

A Note on Measurements

When we convert between American and Metric System measurements, we use rounded-off conversions to provide equivalent levels of precision. Readers familiar with the mathematical concept of significant figures will recognize that these rounded conversions are actually more accurate. Where measurements are only approximate to begin with, as in the nominal gallonage of various standard aquarium sizes, we use only approximate, round conversions.

Of course, measurements, specifically small measurements, are very important when discussing the livestock for nano setups. Of the two systems, American and Metric, the latter is clearly superior for small lengths, so much so that it is common in the United States to indicate very small lengths in millimeters rather than fractions or decimals of inches. The difference between $1^{5}/_{32}$ inches and $1^{1}/_{4}$ inches is not something most people can visualize instantly, while the difference is immediately obvious between 29 mm and 32 mm. The problem of significant figures also looms heavily over trying to compare several measurements all under an inch or two; it is important to remember that $1^{3}/_{4}$ inches and 1.75 inches are not necessarily the same, and while the former can be used to describe an actual measurement of 1.70 inches, the latter cannot.

Also, inch measurements are not conducive to comparing lengths on a continuum. As we talk about small fish, for example, we will be comparing measurements like $1^{1}/_{4}$, $1^{3}/_{4}$, and $2^{1}/_{2}$ inches. On the other hand, millimeters give us a discrete continuum along which we can compare lengths—32, 45, and 64 mm. The animals we will be discussing will range in most cases from about 10 to 60 mm. Therefore, when we note the lengths for a given species, we will indicate them in millimeters, with approximate inch measurements in parentheses, like this: 43 mm (an inch and a half). The Metric figure will be more precise and should be used for comparing two species' lengths.

This is what this book is about: using a small aquarium to take an extremely close look at the marvel of aquatic life. Not all small aquaria fit this description, but aquarists wishing to maintain small tanks for any reason will find a great deal of useful information herein. Nevertheless, our focus is on small tanks set up under the nano concept, from which great enjoyment and satisfaction can be gained.

Time Out
for Betta Bowls

Chapter **2**

As this book celebrates the mini aquarium and tries to share an enthusiasm for desktop aquatic displays of all kinds, it is important to address the modern betta bowl before getting into the subject in depth. Because of their widespread availability and beauty of the males' finnage, bettas have become a fashion item, an ornament for interior decorating. This means that many non-aquarists are keeping bettas, and it means that non-aquarists—often florists—are selling the fish and giving advice about them. Unfortunately, the fish often suffer because of this. At first glance a desktop betta bowl may look like a valid application of the nano concept, and it can be, but many betta bowls are marginally acceptable at best, and some are basically piscine torture chambers. Let's look at why.

Just because bettas can survive in such conditions as shown here doesn't mean they should be subjected to such conditions. Although extreme in nature and probably designed only for photographic artistry, permanently housing a betta in such a small space can cause irreparable damage to the fish.

Betta Bowls

Male *Betta splendens* are available in every color and in a wide variety of fin shapes and sizes. You can actually color-coordinate your betta to your decor. Bettas' ability to breathe air has led to the erroneous conclusion that they need only the smallest volume of water. Many people fail to recognize the similarity of this argument to one nobody would espouse: since dogs breathe air, you can keep one 24-7 in a wire-mesh crate just large enough for the animal to turn around in.

A dog's urine and feces do not disperse and dissolve into the air the way fish wastes do into water, so the unsanitary nature of a fish in a small bowl is not immediately apparent the way a cramped dog crate would be. And, since dogs interact with us much more intimately than fish do, and since it is easier to imagine that dogs have emotions and feelings similar to ours, the cruelty of confining a dog in a small cage is instantly obvious, while the cruelty of tiny betta bowls may not be.

The Betta Bowl Myth

The common betta bowl myth is that these fish can thrive in extremely small volumes of water at room temperature, and their air-breathing is often cited as the reason this is so. Unfortunately for many bettas, this myth is contrary to fact. While oxygen starvation is not a significant consideration for betta bowls, living space, waste dilution, and temperature are.

Since it is possible to find a wild male betta tending his nest in a flooded water buffalo hoofprint, it is obvious that this fish does not need a lot of swimming space. In fact, a male betta living in a much larger body of water defends a very small territory around his nest, which is often anchored to a clump of vegetation.

Consider, however, that many cichlids also stay in a

very small area around their nest sites, but that is not an indication they can be kept in small bowls! When male bettas are kept in regular aquaria, they are not extremely active, but they do prowl around the tank, and there is at least anecdotal evidence that bettas that exercise regularly by swimming fast live much longer than more sedentary specimens.

Waste dilution, though, is a more crucial consideration. A fish in a container of water necessarily swims in and breathes its own wastes. Its body and its delicate gill tissues are bathed in dissolved ammonia, which constantly increases in concentration until the water is changed. Because they obtain oxygen from air, bettas do not die from ammonia-burned gills as quickly as other fishes, but that is not necessarily a benefit. A fish's gills are used for much more than gas exchange. Gill burn will rob a betta of normal osmoregulation and waste elimination functions, enfeebling it and bringing it a premature death from poisoning.

In an established aquarium, ammonia and other wastes are processed into much less harmful substances by beneficial bacteria. This process, known as biofiltration, requires a substrate on which the bacterial colonies can grow. A small bowl does not have sufficient area for these colonies, so toxic levels of wastes are inevitable.

Often a betta bowl is decorated with a substrate of large pebbles or glass beads. These are a poor choice and can be a deadly one. If a morsel of food falls down into the spaces between the stones, the betta will try to extract it, and the fish could wind up stuck if the substrate shifts, trapping its head. If not freed very soon, it will die. If the tidbit falls completely out of the fish's reach, it can still kill the fish, since as pieces of uneaten food accumulate and begin to rot, they can quickly pollute the tank. Even daily water changes will not eliminate this hazard, unless the substrate is completely cleaned with each water change. Regular gravel tubes will probably not be effective, so the rocks need to be removed and cleaned before being put back into the bowl.

The best option in terms of maintaining water quality is to use no substrate, but if a bare-bottom bowl does not appeal to you, use a thin layer (half an inch, or one centimeter) of regular fine aquarium gravel. It still needs to be vacuumed regularly, but that is easy to do, and food cannot sink very far into it in the first place.

Another important factor is temperature. Bettas are tropical fish. Their shallow-water habitats, often without shade, get very warm. A good temperature for bettas is 80°F (27°C), but few people keep their homes that warm. While bettas will survive at room temperature, they will not thrive, and constant chill puts a big stress on the fish and on their immune systems.

The Betta Vase Travesty

The popular "betta vase" takes the betta bowl myth to a further extreme. A glass vase with a narrow neck is fitted with a houseplant whose roots fill the water in which the betta lives. The false logic here is that the plant uses the betta's waste as food, and the betta eats the plant's roots, making a complete ecosystem, a balanced setup that needs no input or output other than light for the plant. A great idea, perhaps, but unfortunately not true.

A plant can certainly remove fish wastes from the water, but it is unlikely that it can remove all of them as fast as they are produced. One benefit of the vase plant, however, is that the roots provide a good medium for bacterial colonization, so a betta vase can have a significant biofilter compared to a bare bowl. On the negative side, the narrow neck of a betta vase raises the real possibility that root growth will block the fish's access to the water surface. If this happens, the betta will asphyxiate, since it is unable to take a breath of air.

Can a Fish Drown?

Although the terminology is sometimes used, fish cannot technically drown, but they may asphyxiate if held under water. Many fish can breathe air to supplement their gill respiration if the oxygen level of the water is too low, but some of these fish are so dependent on air breathing that they will die if they cannot reach the surface.

Probably the cruelest falsehood in the betta vase myth is that bettas eat plant roots. Bettas are principally carnivores. They are micropredators that feed on small invertebrates: worms, insects, crustaceans. A starving betta will certainly peck at plant roots—not to eat them, but to scrape off the microorganisms that grow on and hide among the roots. Since a cold-blooded tropical animal kept at room temperature has a greatly decreased metabolism, and since a vased betta can get some nutrition from microorganisms, it can take a long time for the fish to actually starve to death, by which time its death will probably be attributed to something else.

A Better Betta Bowl

Does this mean that male bettas cannot be kept in a nano display? Absolutely not. Many of the vessels used to house a betta are too small, but the minimum size required depends more on water changes than anything else. A betta bowl with a mere cup (250 ml) of water might be able to house a betta—but only if the water is changed completely at least twice a day. Increasing the volume allows you to safely reduce the rate of water changes, but so does filtration.

Filtration

You are probably aware of the three types of filtration. Of these the most significant one, especially for small volumes, is biological filtration. Mechanical filtration is largely cosmetic and will do little to improve water quality. If you rely on chemical filtration to maintain water quality in a betta bowl, you are flirting with disaster; the first time you are delayed in changing the medium or it becomes exhausted for some other reason, your betta is likely to die of ammonia poisoning. Biofiltration, on the other hand, provides bacterial colonies that can continuously process toxic ammonia and nitrite into nitrate, a less toxic substance whose concentration can be kept low through regular water changes.

This betta has a two-fold problem. If root growth from the plant will block its access to the surface to breathe air. And if the marbles are not removed when cleaning the "substrate," solid wastes and uneaten foots will rot and contaminate the water, resulting in high ammonia levels that will burn the betta's gill tissue. Both issues can lead to the betta's death.

While filtration can only help your betta bowl, one that causes heavy disruption of the water surface will keep you from witnessing one of the most fascinating aspects of keeping a betta: seeing it create a bubble nest!

But how can you install a biofilter in a betta bowl?

We already mentioned biofiltration bacteria growing on a plant's roots. They'll set up house on all submerged parts of a plant, and having even a small Java fern in a bowl can make a big difference. A small sponge filter is ideal, except for its obtrusiveness. That problem is eliminated with a central filtration and flow-through setup for multiple betta bowls, and this design is discussed in Chapter 11, under "Multiple Systems." A simplified version is covered later in this chapter, under "An Easy Alternative."

Heat

Since bettas are best kept at temperatures significantly higher than normal room temperatures, supplemental heat is required for healthy fish. Until recently that has meant using a regular aquarium heater, which even in its smallest incarnation is an eyesore in a desktop betta tank. To make things worse, the lowest-wattage heaters are still so powerful that they cannot produce a steady temperature in a very small volume—the water cools off quickly, causing the heater to come on, but within a very short time it heats back up. At this point the heater shuts off, and even though the small mass of water continues to heat up from the now-cooling heating element, it soon starts to cool off again. In a truly small volume, the betta would be alternately roasted and chilled (see Figure 2.1).

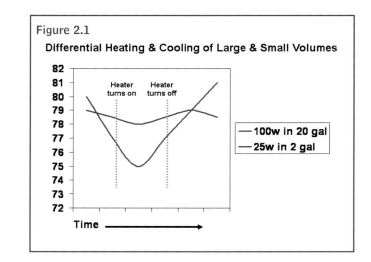

Figure 2.1

Differential Heating & Cooling of Large & Small Volumes

Heater turns on Heater turns off

— 100w in 20 gal
— 25w in 2 gal

Time →

However, manufacturers are now producing tiny heaters designed to be easily concealed in small aquaria. They are of very low wattage, and they are flat, allowing them to be hidden against the back or side glass. Some of these heaters do not have thermostatic control, however, which makes overheating a real concern. A multiple flow-through system also solves the heating problem, since a regular heater can be used in the central sump.

Feeding

A betta in a nano system can certainly be fed as it would be in a regular aquarium. The small volume, however, is easily polluted by even the smallest amount of waste or uneaten food. The problem is exacerbated if gravel is used. Bettas love nothing more than voraciously tearing live or frozen worms or shrimp to pieces, but in their zeal they can make quite a mess. In a larger tank, even if the betta's tankmates did not help pick up the particles that spew around, the greater volume would give much more of a buffer against the pollution of decomposition. A much better solution is to use a small pelleted food as the basis of a betta's diet, with occasional treats of other foods, live, frozen, or freeze dried.

Pellets can be fed one at a time, providing not only portion control but also mess control. If the pellet sinks, the betta will probably catch it before it hits bottom. If it floats, the fish will pick it off the surface. Wait until the betta has completely swallowed the pellet, then offer another. Don't want to pick one tiny pellet at a time out of the package? No problem. You can now buy pellets specifically formulated for bettas; they come in a dispenser that enables you to tap them out singly. Second only to water changes, feeding single pellets is an excellent way to keep the fish healthy and the water clean.

An Easy Alternative

If your betta display is only one of several aquaria that you keep, there is a have-your-cake-and-eat-it-too alternative to the flawed betta bowl. Use a small acrylic tank and position it above another aquarium. It doesn't have to be directly over, but it should be reasonably nearby and at least a couple of inches higher. Drill a hole for a drain at the level you want to maintain the water. Fit a drain (half-inch is large enough) to it and run a drain tube from the bulkhead to the other aquarium. Obtain a small submersible pump whose discharge is less than the diameter of the drain and drain tube. Make sure the pump can handle the head (the height it has to pump water to reach the upper tank). Place the pump in the lower aquarium and run tubing from it up to the betta

Room Temperature Alternatives

There are other fish that are quite comfortable at room temperatures and can be considered instead of a betta for an unheated desktop display. These include white clouds, paradise fish, *Heterandria formosa*, and many killifish.

White cloud, *Tanichthys albonubes*

Killifish, *Aphyosemion celiae*

Paradise fish, *Macropodus opercularis*

A. cameronense

Heterandria formosa

A. ogoense

tank. Secure the tubing to the rim of the tank and start the pump. You now have a circulating system, and the betta tank is heated and filtered by the larger system. If the power goes out or the pump fails, the water will cease flowing up, which will cause the overflow out the drain tube to stop as well. When the power returns, the system will start up on its own. The only caution here is to make sure that the output of the pump does not exceed the volume the drain can handle. If it does, then obviously the betta tank will overflow. It would also be a good idea to put a strainer on the inside of the bulkhead, or cover it with a piece of mesh, to prevent your betta from getting stuck in the drain tube.

There are many other setups that will work, but whatever you choose, remember that bettas need filtered, heated accommodations. Betta bowls and vases *can* be legitimate nano aquaria, but the health and welfare of the fish have to be the driving concerns.

Tank Setup

Chapter **3**

Redrawing the Scale

Size has to be the first consideration when choosing objects and equipment to outfit a nano aquarium. A quarter-inch (6 mm) diameter air hose that can lurk satisfactorily in the corner of a 75-gallon (300-liter) aquarium is often an eyesore anywhere in a desktop setup. An intricately twisted piece of driftwood that would enhance a 20-gallon (80-liter) tank as a centerpiece could overwhelm a 2-gallon (8-liter) aquarium to the point that it looks like a container of wet wood. A modest swordplant among the background planting of a 55-gallon (200-liter) aquarium wouldn't even fit all its leaves into a one-gallon (4-liter) tank.

At the same time, a driftwood chunk that would be overlooked in a 75 could make an intriguing focal point in a desktop tank. A curiously veined rock that would look like an oversized pebble in a 50 might anchor the aquascaping of a 2. And a thicket of *Echinodorus tenellus* (below) that would look like a lawn in a 55 could become a fascinating jungle in a one.

This is where the bonsai mentality comes in. The goal is to design an aquascape in a tiny vessel such that it does not appear cramped or out of scale. The beauty of the nano concept comes from symmetry and balance at the micro level. Foreground plants become background specimens. Near-invisible animals become stars. Gravel pieces become rocks. Rocks become boulders. A

true nano display looks as open, spacious, and uncluttered as any other aquascape.

At first you might think that setting up a nano tank is simply a scaled-down version of setting up any other aquarium, just using fewer items. Such an approach, however, results in one of those ho-hum disappointments. You wind up with a tank in which everything, substrate, decor, even the plants and fish, appear crowded—the maple seedling in a pot. But with careful planning and choice, the same tank can be outfitted with miniature substrate, tiny decor, and diminutive plants and fish to present a spacious and dynamic display—the bonsai tree. A successful nano aquarium produces the same sense of space and motion that a large display tank does, only on a miniature scale.

Obviously the first thing to consider is the aquarium itself. There are many possibilities, both vessels intended as aquaria and those manufactured for other purposes. Let's look at some of the possibilities and discuss them in terms of the nano concept.

Material

Glass and acrylic are the usual choices for material. Acrylic is easier to form into various shapes, but some amazing things are being done with glass as well. The greater thermal insulation of plastic will greatly help offset the heat loss problems of mini aquaria, but both plastic and glass are serviceable. The usual comparisons are that plastic is lighter, stronger, clearer, and a better insulator, while glass is cheaper, more scratch resistant, and heavier—which in the case of a small desktop aquarium can be a benefit.

A unique nano aquarium could follow the original vessels used by the ancient Chinese to display goldfish: low, wide ceramic bowls. The early strains of goldfish were intended to be viewed from above, so the fish were kept in such containers. Although goldfish are a poor choice for any small aquarium, the idea can be applied to any suitably small species. Any fish takes on a very different appearance when seen only from above, and many interesting nano setups are possible using glass or glazed pottery bowls, urns, and basins. Heating and filtering such vessels, however, is problematic.

Size Limits

Just how big—or small—is a nano aquarium? Because the nano aquarium concept is as much philosophy as application, it is not possible to give a strictly numerical definition of a nano tank. This is true in both directions: we cannot say that an aquarium of a certain size is definitely a nano tank, and we cannot say that an aquarium of a certain size is too large to be a nano tank. Moreover, within our definition one way of setting up a given aquarium might be considered a nano system, while another might not.

That said, in most cases the aquaria we will be discussing will be 10 gallons (40 liters) or less, but the concept can be extended into larger tanks. This is especially true with all-in-one units, which are commonly available in a range of sizes from a few gallons up to 25 or 30 gallons (from several liters up to 100 liters) or even more.

There really is no minimum size for a nano aquarium. If the nano concept is properly implemented, the livestock in the vessel will always be scaled to the amount of water. A 2-cup (500-ml) bowl stocked with a single newborn guppy, a small ramshorn snail, and a sprig of hornwort *Ceratophyllum* is a perfectly viable display, while a 2-gallon (8-liter) tank with a 2-inch (5-cm) comet goldfish is not.

A ramshorn snail.

Shape

Aquaria of all sizes exist in a wide array of shapes, some more fanciful than practical. Several things other than aesthetics are affected by a tank's shape. For example, a drum or spherical bowl is narrowest at the bottom and top. The maximum diameter is at the equator, so filling the bowl halfway provides much more surface area for gas exchange. That is a special case, and most shapes provide a constant surface area from top to bottom. Even so, the shape has a profound effect on what that surface area is.

Footprint

The footprint of a tank—the size and shape of its supported surface—is important in two ways. Almost all aquaria have the same size top surface as bottom surface. Since gas exchange—oxygen in, carbon dioxide out—takes place primarily at the water surface, the larger the surface area, the better the gas exchange, and the more fish the tank can support.

Consider two aquaria, one with a footprint of one foot (30 cm) by one foot (30 cm) and a height of 4 feet (120 cm), the other with a two- by two-foot (60- by 60-cm) footprint and a height of one foot (30 cm). Both tanks (see Figure 3.1) hold about 30 gallons (110 liters) of water, but the surface area of the shorter one is four times that of the other and so offers four times the gas exchange. Such limitations can partially be overcome with aeration—mechanical movement of the water to constantly refresh the surface. The larger surface area remains an advantage, however, even if only as an asset during a power failure.

Figure 3.1

The larger the footprint the more surface space available for gas exchange.

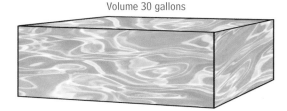

2 ft x 2 ft x 1 ft tall
4 sq ft footprint
Volume 30 gallons

1 ft x 1 ft x 4 ft tall
1 sq ft footprint
Volume 30 gallons

Many popular standard American aquarium sizes share the same footprint and surface areas:

Nominal Gallons	Footprint in Inches
10, 15-high	12 x 20
15, 20-high, 25	12 x 24
20-long, 29, 37	12 x 30
30, 38, 45	12 x 36
33-long, 40, 55	13 x 48
30-breeder, 40-breeder, 50, 65	36 x 18

The other significance of a tank's footprint is in bottom surface area. Territorial species, especially fish that inhabit and defend a hole or cave, typically set up home on the tank bottom. Many cichlids, catfish, and loaches are in this category, and a tank's footprint determines how many territories can be set up, and therefore how many fish the tank can hold. In the above example, the wide, short aquarium has four times the room for such territories as the thin, tall one.

Height

Aside from its role in determining volume, the height of an aquarium is important in itself. The primary viewing panel of most tanks is the front glass, so the left-to-right length and the height of the aquarium determine the size and shape of this viewing surface. In most configurations, increased height leads to an increased aesthetic value. The extremely popular 55-gallon (200-liter) aquarium has many disadvantages relating to its narrowness front-to-back, but the viewing panel is 48 inches by 20 inches (120 by 50 cm), the same as that of the more adaptable 75-gallon (300-liter) tank. The 55's shortcomings are for many people made up for by its pleasing presentation.

Different Footprints

Both the 55-gallon (200-liter) and the 75-gallon (300-liter) tanks have the same size front glass: 48 by 20 inches (120 by 50 cm). Their footprints, however, differ: 48 by 13 (120 by 33 cm) for the 55, and 48 by 18 inches (120 by 46 cm) for the 75.

Maintaining a constant water temperature is essential for your fish, especially saltwater species. While some freshwater species, like *Tanichthys albonubes,* can survive at room temperature or cooler, saltwater species like these *Amphiprion percula* cannot. Percula clowns, and other saltwater fishes, come from coral reefs, where the temperature rarely changes.

Height is a concern in aquarium setup and maintenance. In very deep tanks it can be difficult to arrange the decor or vacuum the gravel. Water circulation is also a problem. It takes an extraordinarily powerful air pump to overcome the water pressure in a tank deeper than 2 feet (60 cm), and any power filter or pump near the surface would have a hard time moving the water near the bottom. Temperature and dissolved oxygen stratification are real possibilities as well. On the nano scale, it can be very difficult to service tall, thin, columnar or cylindrical aquaria, and there is little swimming room in them for the fish.

Thermal Stability

Marine and freshwater setups share a physical concern relating to size that directly affects a nano tank: relative heat loss. This is one argument for starting big in the aquarium hobby, whether fresh or marine. A body's heat loss is determined by its total surface area, a square measurement, while its heat content is determined by its volume, a cubic measurement. If dimensions are tripled, area goes up by a factor of 9, but volume increases by a factor of 27. Thus, if we have two aquaria at the same temperature, one three times the dimensions of the other, the larger one has 27 times the volume of the smaller one, but only 9 times its surface area. So, the smaller tank heats up or cools off three times as quickly as the larger one does.

All-in-One Units

The concept of an integral aquarium system has been around for a long time, but we can again thank the reef aquarium hobby for the current proliferation of such units and especially for the popular cubic design. The minimal application of this concept is an aquarium hood with integral lighting and filtration. The most complex "reef ready" units incorporate lighting, filtration, heating, cooling, surface skimming, water pumps, and even moon lighting in the hood and the back compartment of the unit. A bit pricey for a simple nano setup, these aquaria are very popular with both reef aquarists and aquatic gardeners, both of whom make regular use of the types of high-intensity lighting these units include.

The cubic design also appeals to these two groups because of the mathematical fact that a square maximizes the footprint area of the tank. Since it is the size of the footprint that determines the number of plants or reef invertebrates that can be placed into the aquarium, a square design provides the maximum area for aquarist to fill. Of course, it also minimizes the length of the aquarium, but since fish are secondary in a planted tank or a reef setup, as well as typically small, the loss of swimming room is an acceptable tradeoff.

There are less elaborate integral units that incorporate lighting and a simple power filter into the hood. These are available as complete units with an acrylic tank or as the hood unit alone, which can fit onto various standard-size aquaria.

Thermal stability is of great significance for ultra small aquaria. Heaters for these tanks must be very low wattage because the water will heat up very quickly when the heating element turns on. They must also be very precise, since the water cools off very quickly once the element goes off, and the heater needs to come on as soon as the temperature drops and turn off before the water overheats. As mentioned in the previous chapter, there are now very small wattage heaters available that are easy to place and to conceal in a nano aquarium. The low power of these units helps greatly to stabilize the water temperature and avoid unsafe swings up and down as the heater cycles on and off. Unfortunately, some do not have thermostats and are always on. If such a unit is adequate for the tank, a rise in the room temperature could result in a tragic overheating of the water, and if it is inadequate, it will fail to maintain the proper water temperature despite it's being always on.

You will see various recommendations in terms of watts per gallon (or liter) for aquarium heaters. The differential heat loss of small tanks reveals the inappropriateness of such recommendations. More accurate is the advice to figure about 5 watts per gallon (about 1½ watts per liter) for small tanks and 2 to 3 watts per gallon (a half to three-quarters watts per liter) for large tanks. Ambient conditions, such as cold rooms or nighttime heat shutoffs, can necessitate more powerful heaters. The smallest nano systems will be very precarious in terms of thermal stability, and maintaining the proper temperature range is a much more significant concern than it is with larger aquaria.

Filtration

There are basically four options for filtering a nano aquarium, not including having no filter, which is almost never a good idea.

Undergravel Filter

The tried-and-true undergravel filter (UGF) is a reasonable option for the nano tank. In fact, the manufacturers of many desktop aquaria include an integral UGF in the system. The only visible component is the riser tube, and despite the

This UGF is being installed underneath a crushed coral substrate.

controversy surrounding them, UGFs are excellent biofilters. The major objections to them are especially easily dismissed in a nano system. Specifically:

- Nano fish are unlikely to dig down to the plate, interrupting the water flow.
- It is a simple matter to clean under the plate by periodically inserting a piece of air tubing down the riser and under the plate, then siphoning.
- The relatively low volume turnover with an airlift suits a small tank perfectly.

Air Driven Sponge Filter

An air driven sponge filter has many attributes. It is inexpensive, easy to maintain, and efficient, providing mechanical and biological filtration. It has no moving parts to break and will survive years and years of constant use. It even provides a perfect substrate for the growth of various microorganisms which fry and other small fish find delectable. So, why not simply recommend an air driven sponge filter for all nano setups?

Simple: they're ugly.

Sponge filters are widely used in fishrooms and hatcheries—sometimes every single aquarium is filtered by them. On the other hand, very, very few display aquaria contain sponge filters, except outside the aquarium in the form of sponge media in power or canister filters. In a larger tank, it might be possible to place plants or other items to block the filter from view, but in a nano setup it is going to be obtrusive at best.

Scaled Down Power Filter

One of the most exciting pieces of equipment to become available is the nano sized power filter. These minute filters hang on the back of the tank and include an appropriately sized water pump. Since everything is miniature, so is the current produced, meaning you can enjoy the benefits of a power filter with various media without your fish being buffeted around the tank.

Refugium Filtration

The use of a refugium has become very popular among some marine aquarists. In extreme cases the refugium is many times the volume of the display tank. An aquarist with

Not All Inches Are Created Equal

Many people add up "fish inches" to decide the stocking capacity of an aquarium. The assumption is that two 3-inch (8-cm) fish somehow equal one 6-inch (16-cm) fish. It is a false assumption. The major factors to consider in terms of stocking capacity are metabolic—such things as oxygen requirement and waste production. These depend on body mass, on how much fish flesh there is in each fish in the aquarium. A tank that can support ten 1-inch or 1-cm fish is not necessarily adequate for a single 10-inch or 10-cm specimen. In fact, a 10-unit fish has roughly 1,000 times the body mass of a 1-unit fish, or 100 times the mass of a school of ten 1-unit fish!

a 5-unit (gallon, liter, etc.) tank plumbed into a 100-unit refugium only has to buy livestock for the 5 but has 105 units of water for chemical and thermal stability. In the previous chapter we discussed an alternative for a betta display that involved refugium filtration—a small betta tank was plumbed into a larger aquarium, whose heating and filtration also served the betta setup. This idea is expandable to service any number of nano setups plumbed together serially. Once their total volume begins to approach that of the refugium you will need to increase the heating and filtration on that tank, or consider moving either to a central filtration and heating system with a sump (basically a refugium without livestock in it) or a canister filter.

Cycling

I stated up front that this book is geared primarily for an aquarist with some experience, but the controversy and confusion surrounding the most basic of aquarium concepts, cycling, pervades all levels of the hobby. As should be obvious by now, the small volume of a nano system makes proper cycling even more important, since the margin for error is so much smaller. On the other hand, the small size of the fish kept in a nano system means the bioload is going to be lighter.

The concept of cycling has undergone a lot of evolution since it was first brought up in the hobby half a century ago. One of the earliest articles I can personally remember advised starting a marine tank by adding some chopped clams and waiting until they rotted away before adding any fish. Apparently that very practical advice was ahead of its time and was met with little enthusiasm, and we saw a lot of different recipes for cycling before things came full circle; today most serious hobbyists recommend cycling without live fish, using a hunk of fish meat…or chopped clams!

There is, however, an even better method. Although people talk about *cycling an aquarium*, the process actually involves *maturing a biofilter*. Since the amount of fish flesh in a nano tank is typically small, a relatively small biofilter is all that is required, though it must be mature, stable, and ready to handle the ammonia production of the tank inhabitants. A good way of providing this is to mature the filter on an established aquarium and then transfer it to its intended tank.

If your biofilter is going to be an undergravel filter, you should set up the nano tank with gravel from an established aquarium. It would be best if the source aquarium is also operating with a UGF, since the bacterial colonies will be more fully established. In most cases gravel from an established tank will be well colonized and will quickly establish a functional biofilter in any case. This is where the small total bioload of a nano aquarium is an asset, since the required biofilter will be proportionally small as well.

If the filter is going to be a sponge or power filter, it should be matured on an established tank—preferably a crowded one—for six weeks. Fish should be placed into the nano aquarium when the filter is moved to it, since running a seasoned filter on an empty tank will quickly cause the bacterial colonies to crash from starvation.

Another option is to load a power filter with media from an established filter. The modular nature of many power filter medium components may make this impossible, however.

Whatever method you choose to establish a biofilter, the biofilter needs to be mature before you stock your tank with fish—or complete your stocking if you are cycling with a few hardy fish or by the gradual, one-fish-at-a-time method.

Safety Considerations

Safety is a concern with absolutely any aquarium setup, and many factors are the same for nano tanks as for larger ones, while a few are quite different.

Electrical Safety

The fact that desktop aquaria are less out of the way than many larger setups, coupled with the cramped quarters in which to house all the equipment, makes it more likely for accidents to occur with the smaller tanks. Practically all aquarium systems mix electrical

Shocking!

You may hear discussion of stray current in aquarium circles. The idea is that minor electrical leakage charges the water with very small electrical currents that harm the fish. Aquarists can detect these currents via mild shocks they receive when they put their hands into the water. These currents are blamed for a variety of ills, including head and lateral line erosion. The problem is that aquarium water—and the fish in it—are not grounded; therefore electricity cannot flow through them. Like a bird perched on a 20,000-volt high tension wire, the electricity cannot affect them. Neither a circuit breaker nor a GFI device can eliminate the possibility of stray currents, but if you use a GFI device and a grounding probe, any stray current that develops should trip the GFI, alerting you to the problem. Without the probe, the current doesn't happen until you stick in your hand and thereby ground the tank.

equipment with water. This raises two concerns in addition to potential damage to the equipment: keeping water out of the appliances and preventing electrocution in case it gets in anyway.

The first concern is properly addressed with three precautions:

• Use only equipment manufactured for aquarium use.

• Use the equipment unaltered, and only for the purposes intended.

• Create drip loops on all wires plugged into electrical outlets.

In the event a non-submersible appliance falls into the water, or if something breaks, exposing inner parts to water, unplug the device before attempting to rectify things. All together, these precautions will prevent most electrocution hazards by preventing the electrification of the aquarium water. This, however, is not sufficient. You must also protect yourself, your friends, and your family in the event that a short does develop, putting your aquarium's water in direct contact with a live electrical circuit.

This protection is easily supplied with a ground fault interrupting (GFI) circuit breaker. This can be a main breaker in your electrical service panel, which protects anything plugged into any outlet on this circuit, or it can be a GFI power strip or a GFI outlet wired in place of a standard duplex outlet, in which case it will protect anything

Special Nano Concerns

They say a picture is worth a thousand words. Well, consider this verbal painting and take heed: a beautiful desktop aquarium sits on a desk next to a folder holding the year's income tax receipts. The tank has a power compact light, a miniature submersible heater, and an airstone. Several fish swim happily through live plants. Enter an unaccompanied two-year-old. Moments later the light fixture is dangling over the edge of the desk by its cord and the heater lies on the desk. The air pump is disconnected, and water is siphoning out through the airline onto the folder of tax receipts. The child is trying to catch the fish by hand and rips the plants out and throws them on the floor in frustration. A final lunge slides the tank to the edge of the desk, where it teeters as the toddler, now bored, scampers off the desk and out the door. The overheated heater tube ignites a box of tissues on the desk just as the aquarium loses its battle with gravity. The sound of splintering glass on the tile floor brings adults running just as the smoke alarm sounds. . .

plugged into that outlet. The law requires electrical use in kitchens, bathrooms, swimming pools, and other wet environments to be protected by GFI devices. It is only common sense that you protect aquarium use of electricity in the same way.

Many people do not understand GFI protection, nor understand its importance. Regular circuit breakers protect against fire and the destruction of electrical equipment. They will not, however, protect against electrocution *unless and until the amperage running through someone's body exceeds the capacity of the wiring to handle the load.* This is usually 20 amps, and at 120 volts, by that point the victim is already long dead.

GFI breakers, on the other hand, interrupt the current the instant there is a ground fault, that is, as soon as the current running from the power supply exceeds that returning to the service panel through the neutral wire. In practical terms: a GFI device shuts off the electricity if the current starts running through you instead of through an electrical appliance. If you're lucky, this will happen quickly enough to spare you a tragedy.

GFI breakers can very well save your life.

A further level of protection can be provided by grounding the aquarium. A titanium grounding rod can be secured in the tank with a wire from it to a grounded site—often a metal water pipe or the center screw on a grounded duplex outlet. This setup will cause a GFI breaker to trip as soon as a ground fault develops and current starts flowing through the probe to ground. Without the ground, the water, insulated by silicone and glass, remains charged, waiting for you or a family member to touch it and complete the circuit to ground.

Stability Concerns

An empty aquarium is heavy, but water is even heavier. Figure approximately 10 pounds per gallon total for a setup (you need to figure more than a kilo per liter in order to take into account the weight of the tank and equipment). In other words, a 10-gallon system weighs about 100 pounds (40 liters, 50 kg), and a 100-gallon tank strains your floor to the tune of a half ton (400 liters, 500 kg)! This is why you should use only stands manufactured specifically for your size aquarium, and never use regular furniture like a desk or a table to hold an aquarium larger than 10 gallons.

With nano systems, however, the concern is more that they are not very heavy. If you have a 75-gallon (300-liter) tank next to your desk and you bump your elbow into it reaching for something, the only consequences will probably be a sore elbow and some startled fish. Bump into a desktop aquarium, and you may knock it over or even off the

Do not underestimate the weight of an aquarium. It is heavier than you may think.

desk onto the floor. These tanks should be placed as much out of the way as possible, preferably not on the edge of the furniture. Likewise, since fish are easily spooked, and since glass breaks easily and even acrylic will crack under sufficient impact, an aquarium should never be located where it is likely to be crashed into by opening doors, children's playthings, or normal household traffic.

Chemical Hazards

Although a leaking aquarium can ruin a great deal of carpeting or other flooring, it poses little chemical threat to the occupants of a home. Normal household activities, however, can present considerable toxic danger to the occupants of an aquarium.

Dust and oily aerosols can settle on the water surface; then even if the substance is not toxic, it can interfere with gas exchange. In addition, anything that is sprayed, dusted, or rubbed onto people, clothing, or furniture in the house has the potential of winding up dissolved in the aquarium water. Many of these products are hazardous to

Infections

You should be aware that waterborne bacteria can enter any open sore on your skin; on rare occasions aquarists get some nasty infections that way.

aquatic life. Especially dangerous are insecticides and other products which carry a warning about human inhalation (paints, solvents, adhesives, etc.); these are harmful to fish at even lower concentrations. Tobacco smoke is poisonous to fish, but your health and that of your family is a much better reason to forego smoking.

Chemicals on your hands—soaps, detergents, lotions, perfumes—can contaminate the water in any aquarium, but the relatively small volume of a nano system means much higher concentrations can result from even minimal contact. The best solution is to wear plastic or rubber gloves when servicing inside the aquarium, but a good alternative is to wash your hands well and then to rinse them several times with plain water to remove any trace of soap before placing your hands into the tank.

In a marine nano setup, the substrate must be deep enough to allow jawfish to burrow.

Special Maintenance Concerns

In Chapter 7 we will discuss many concerns in maintaining stability in a nano setup in the context of marine systems. Those apply—though less significantly—to freshwater systems, so rather than list them here as well, I'll just recommend that even no-salt aquarists should read over that section to glean what applies. What follows here applies to both freshwater and marine systems equally.

Solvent-Solute Ratio

A small volume of water has certain benefits when it comes to aquarium maintenance, as well as certain disadvantages. Often both stem from the same factor: solvent-solute ratio. The solvent in an aquarium is the universal solvent, water. Everything that dissolves into the water is a solute. In a nano system, there is a very small volume of solvent. It follows that there should be equally diminutive amounts of solutes in the tank.

This creates a problem when we consider dissolved wastes. The amount of wastes generated by a given fish in one day is the same no matter what size tank it swims in. We can call that amount x. In a week that fish will produce 7x. If its aquarium contains 1.0 gallon (3.8 liters) of water, at the end of the first week there will be 7x in that water, at a concentration of $7x/1 = 7x$ per gallon ($7x/3.8 = 1.8x$ per liter), but if the tank contains 20.0 gallons (76 liters) of water, the concentration will be only $7x/20 = 0.35x$ per gallon ($7x/76 = 0.09x$ per liter), a mere 5 percent of the concentration in the nano aquarium.

Aside from aesthetics, this is the major reason that nano aquarium inhabitants have to be tiny. Large animals simply produce too much waste to be effectively dissolved in the volume of water in a nano tank, no matter how much filtration or water changing you supply.

The other side of this is the small amount of a particular solute you need to maintain it at a certain concentration in a nano tank. This comes into play when you consider the cost of medicating the tank or the cost of marine salt mix for water changes. Likewise, if you want to doctor your tap water to achieve a specific chemistry for your nano system, you will need much less additive, medium, or treatment than you'd need for a larger tank. But wait. There's a down side to this as well.

Since tiny amounts of solute can make a big difference in concentration when the volume of solvent is small, it is much easier to get the concentration wrong in a nano system. If you are off by a few spoonfuls of salt mix or a couple drops of chemicals in a 100-gallon (400-liter) tank, the resultant concentration might not be measurably different from what it would have been if you had added the precise amount. In a one-gallon (4-liter) tank, however, it could make a significant difference. In fact, even just getting the correct dosage in the first place may be difficult. What would you do, for instance, with an additive that is to be added at the rate of one drop per 10 gallons? So, while adjusting water chemistry in a nano setup definitely requires much less expense in terms of the salt or other chemical additives needed, it also requires much more accuracy in measuring the additives. In some cases the level of precision needed may be beyond your ability to provide.

Keeping to Scale

A nano setup suffers greatly as soon as the nano scale is compromised. For example, while deep sandbeds of even 6 inches (15 cm) or more work very well in large tanks, even an inch or so (3 cm) of sand or gravel can overwhelm a tiny aquarium, since a disproportionately large fraction of the total height is occupied by the substrate. The particle size of gravel is also significant; coarse gravel will in itself make a very small tank look crowded, and sand or very fine gravel will work much better.

We've already mentioned using plants with small stems and leaves. Complete nano aquacapes can be made with traditional "foreground" plants (see Figure 3.2)—dwarf *Sagittaria* and *Vallisneria, Lillaeopsis*, and *Glossostigma*. The same effect a raft of floating water sprite *Ceratopteris difformis* makes in a large aquarium can be made in miniature with a portion of duckweed *Lemna* sp. in a nano setup. Instead of large *Echinodorus* swords for centerpieces, try *Anubias nana*. Twig-like pieces of driftwood can serve as branches.

Keep the bonsai idea in mind; if someone were to view a photo of your tank with no size reference, it should not be easy for him or her to notice that it is a nano setup. This avoids the crowded look that plagues many small aquaria. The person looking at the photo should have no point of reference for size. Perhaps you have seen demonstrations of an Ames Room, wherein false visual cues make it appear that people standing in the room are of vastly different size; in fact, as subjects walk through the room, they appear to grow or shrink in front of your eyes. Although not intended to be an optical illusion, a nano tank should in part fool the eye. Without a reference point, the tank will look like a much larger one. When a photo of the tank tricks the eye, the actual aquarium will seem spacious and well-designed—a miniature aquascape, not an aquascape crammed into a small space.

Figure 3.2

Traditional "Foreground" Plants

Anubias nana

Glossostigma elatinoides

Sagittaria platyphylla

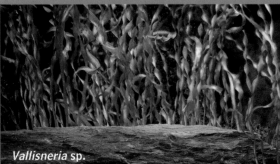

Vallisneria sp.

Health Concerns

Chapter 4

This is not a typical chapter on fish health. We are not going to go through lists of diagnoses and treatments. Some of the reasons for this are:

- Fish are tough. Most aquarium species are extremely hardy as long as they are not mistreated or unduly stressed.
- Prevention works much better than cure. While it is extremely easy to prevent most fish disease outbreaks, it is extremely difficult to successfully treat most fish disease outbreaks.
- We are not veterinarians. If you had a friend who was always giving her dog or cat injections, you'd probably suggest that she seek the advice of a trained professional. Unfortunately, people don't usually equate this with dumping antibiotics and other drugs into their fish tanks. Dosing any animal without complete knowledge of the effects, side effects, and interactions of different medicines is very dangerous.
- Successful aquarists rarely have disease problems, and when they do, they tend not to use drugs to treat their fish.

Getting Sick

There are only two ways a fish—or any other animal—can fall ill, whether to an infection from bacteria or viruses or from an infestation of parasites: it can be exposed to a pathogen, or it can suffer a reduced immune response due to stress and thereby succumb to a pathogen already present. To make these concepts more real, let's look at some human parallels.

When Europeans colonized the New World, they certainly were in many instances aggressive toward the native peoples they encountered, but the most deadly weapons they unleashed upon the indigenes were ones they carried in their bodies. (European diseases were

Due to the smaller sizes of a nano aquarium, hobbyists must monitor the tank's water parameters more stringently than they would a much larger tank. There is little room for error.

especially virulent, since they evolved in crowded urban centers. Under less crowded conditions, such diseases die out after affecting a group of people before they can be passed on to another group.) Europeans had considerable immunity to the diseases that had been circulating in European cities for centuries. Some of these immunities were hard-won, with diseases like smallpox occasionally wiping out whole families. Nevertheless, the people who survived to cross the Atlantic were largely immune to many terrible diseases, and their children born in the Americas had some genetic immunity that often enabled them to survive outbreaks even if they became ill.

The people living in the New World, however, had never been exposed to these pathogens. They carried no genetic resistance to them, and they had no acquired immunity from earlier exposure. Typhus, measles, smallpox, influenza, and many other diseases would rip through their villages, often leaving 100 percent of the people dead. In the first 100 years of European colonization, between 85 and 90 percent of all native American peoples had been exterminated by European diseases. This is greater than the Nazi extermination of two-thirds of European Jewry and far greater than the Black Death's extermination of half of Europe's population or Pol Pot's genocide of 25 percent of Cambodian citizens.

Now think about your aquarium. The fish in it are all healthy. Let's suppose they are all from a fish farm that sterilizes each pond between batches of fish and makes sure no wild fish contaminate their ponds. Now you bring in some new fish from a less stringent fish farm—or maybe even the wild. If you place the new fish directly in with your other fish, and they are carrying pathogens, chances are good that in a short time all of your original fish will be dead. If instead you quarantine the new fish long enough for any latent diseases to manifest themselves, you can save your entire collection. Although we hope to successfully treat any quarantined fish that becomes ill, if the ailment proves incurable at least only the one fish is lost, not all the fish in the main tank.

Minding Ps and Qs

The key, then, to keeping your fish healthy is to mind your Ps and Qs—to practice prevention and quarantine.

Prevention

I've already mentioned that fish are naturally hardy. As long as they are not subjected to too many stressors, they can usually resist most pathogens. Fortunately, to avoid stress fish do not have to go on vacation or get help paying the bills. All they require is

an environment that does not interfere with their everyday needs. Those needs are typically quite simple:

- Appropriate water chemistry. For most species this means clean water free from dissolved wastes and without sanitizing chemicals such as chlorine and chloramine.
- Proper diet. In most cases this means a variety of foods to cover any deficiencies in one or another of them, with attention to the fish's natural diet in terms of herbivory, carnivory, or omnivory, and in appropriate amounts.
- Adequate infrastructure.
- A bit of peace.

While these factors are the same for fish in setups of any size, there are special nano concerns and ramifications for each. It is not difficult to meet these everyday needs of your fish.

- The easiest way to provide clean water for your nano fish on a long-term basis is to change the water frequently. Filtration is important, especially biofiltration, but the small volume of a nano setup begs for this easy way out. Think of the aquarium as a temporary vessel for water between changes.
- The micro nature of a nano setup necessitates special diligence to make sure the small amount of food needed is of the highest quality and that the quantity is carefully regulated to prevent overfeeding the aquarium and polluting the water.
- Tiny fish require tiny refuges. The nano aquascape should contain plenty of nano-sized hide holes and caverns. Plant thickets provide natural cover.
- Easily spooked species, of course, are not candidates for a nano tank, no matter how small they are. Still, a nano setup should be situated so that it does not receive undue disturbance from household traffic or activities. And don't forget that there is literally no room for a territorial bully in a tiny tank, in which other fish simply cannot get away from the aggressor.
- Meeting your fish's basic needs will alleviate stress, and lack of stress allows their immune systems to function properly.

Quarantine

If your fish are not infected, and they aren't stressed, then preventing new pathogens from entering the system should avoid disease outbreaks. How do you prevent your fish from coming into contact with new pathogens? In a word: quarantine.

Many people think of quarantine only in terms of isolating newly acquired specimens before letting them join your collection to keep pathogens out of your main system. While this is vitally important, there are other considerations. Whether wild caught or farm raised, your new fish undergo a stressful journey to get to your local retailer. Along the way they are subjected to stressful changes in water chemistry and temperature. They may also be netted, attacked by other fish, or handled roughly in transport. Thus they arrive in

If you notice an illness or serious injury, you should move your fish to a quarantine (hospital) tank. Keeping it separate from your main tank can prevent further spread of the illness in your main tank, and time to heal without stress from interactions with healthy, active tankmates.

your home exhausted, nervous, hungry, and otherwise stressed. Quarantine gives the new fish time to relax and recuperate before having to face the stress of entering an established community and fighting for a position in the pecking order.

A quarantine tank need not be large or elaborate. If you keep an extra sponge filter bubbling in an aquarium, it will always have a mature biofilter when you need to move it into the quarantine tank. A piece of PVC pipe or a bunch of plastic plants can provide an easy-to-clean hideaway. A bare-bottom aquarium is best, since it enables you to keep the tank very clean with regular siphoning. Lighting is unimportant, and in most cases the ambient light in the room is sufficient—preferable in fact, since a dimly lit tank decreases stress on the fish. It is a good idea to keep the water a few degrees warmer than in your regular tanks, as warmth helps healing.

How long should quarantine last? Many people feel a week or two is sufficient. Certainly many illnesses will manifest themselves within that time. Some, however, will not. The life cycle of many pathogens can take a month or more to complete. It is safest to consider four to six weeks the proper interval for quarantine. Quarantine is one corner most of us cut at some time, and some people get away with it for a long time. But eventually disaster will strike. It always seems this takes place when the victims are especially beloved or expensive specimens. Learn your lesson from others' mistakes, and quarantine your new arrivals.

The Hospital Tank

Sometimes, despite our efforts in quarantine and prevention, fish are injured or become ill. Then it is time to use your quarantine tank—this time as a hospital tank.

A separate tank can double as a quarantine and a hospital tank.

Treating fish in any setup is problematic, but in a nano aquarium it is even more so. Treatments wreck havoc with plants, invertebrates, and biofilters. If you use natural methods like salinity manipulation and raising the temperature, the damage may not be as severe as with chemical medications, but all are destructive. It makes no sense to heal a fish while simultaneously killing off plants or biofiltration bacteria.

Almost any minor ailment of aquarium fish can be treated successfully by increasing the temperature and changing salinity. For freshwater fish you add salt, for marine fish you lower the salinity by mixing in fresh water. The idea behind this is that microorganisms and small parasites cannot handle the osmotic stress and are killed either by bursting (marine organism in low salinity) or desiccating (freshwater organism in salty water). In fact, a more aggressive protocol calls for manipulating the salinity in the hospital tank and giving daily baths—freshwater baths for marine fish, saltwater baths for freshwater fish. The fish is placed into the bath for one to two minutes once or twice a day.

A large water change should be made every day in the hospital tank, with a thorough vacuuming of the bare bottom. This greatly reduces the number of pathogens in the tank and bolsters the sick fish by keeping water conditions especially pristine.

Wounds

A fish wounded in an accident or by a tankmate will usually heal quickly without treatment. A torn fin or a few missing scales are soon repaired or replaced. Fish can even regrow entire fins. Occasionally, however, a wound will become infected. The flesh becomes swollen and red, or covered with a cottony growth. Salinity manipulation is usually sufficient to aid the fish in recovering.

Invertebrate Health Concerns

The same regimen of regular water changes and proper diet and an appropriate environment free of stress that is discussed in this chapter for fish also applies to any invertebrates kept in a nano tank. If you take care of your aquarium it will thrive, whether you house vertebrates or inverts, freshwater, salt, or brackish.

Spots

The most common diseases encountered by aquarists are parasites (ich, velvet, blackspot) and often respond well to the regimen just described. Advanced or stubborn cases may require the use of chemicals. Most of the traditional medications for aquarium fish are hazardous substances that are now strictly controlled. You should consult your local dealer or veterinarian for information about safe and legal treatments for the problems you are having.

Coral—such as this *Ricordea florida*, or orange Florida ricordia mushroom—benefit from a regimen of frequent water changes. Such regimens will keep your nano aquarium healthy and vibrant, regardless of what you keep in it.

Several Sad Truths

There is a common misconception that modern medicine, whether human or veterinary, can "fix" anything that goes wrong. Many people are angry when the pediatrician refuses to prescribe antibiotics for their children's colds and sore throats. The truth, however, is that viral diseases cannot be cured with medicine, and useless prescriptions lead only to medical problems and drug-resistant microbes.

Sadder still is the truth that an antibiotic bath does little good, even for fish afflicted with bacteria susceptible to the antibiotic. The best way to administer such a drug to a fish is to inject it. In fact, many owners of koi and other large, expensive fish do seek out a veterinarian to treat their sick fish, but for the average aquarist this route is too expensive. Often the purchase price of an entire tankful of fish is less than it would cost to treat a single specimen. And, it gets worse when you consider that the lack of research into the medical problems of aquarium species means that even with professional care many fish ailments are untreatable.

In summary, it is unfortunate, but except for the most common ones, fish diseases are effectively untreatable. The happy truth, however, is that they are for the most part preventable. Most advanced hobbyists have little experience with disease—because they mind their Ps and Qs. You should, too.

Freshwater Fishes

Chapter 5

In most cases, only fish under 2 inches (5 cm) can be candidates for a nano tank, though small size is a necessary but not sufficient attribute for a good nano fish. For example, many otherwise nicely diminutive danios have too frenetic a lifestyle for most aquaria of desktop size. They display naturally only in large schools—a dozen or more. Even in a tank as large as 10 gallons (40 liters), a school of danios will give the impression of being cramped as they dash back and forth, hampered by the ever-present glass walls. Similarly, a slightly larger but sedentary fish might be perfectly acceptable for a nano display.

On the other hand, wall-hung aquaria have appeared on the market. These are extremely thin tanks (less than 6 inches/15 cm) that are basically all viewing panel and hold only a few gallons. The nano nature of these aquaria is evident in the giant version—a 7-foot-long (180-cm) model that holds only 30 gallons (120 liters). What better fish for such a tank than a school of danios? Their small size makes them suitable for the small volume, but the length of the aquarium provides plenty of swimming and schooling space. Once again, stocking such a tank with "normal" species will result in stifled and cramped fish, while a nano design will recreate in a low-volume tank the type of dynamic display found in much larger community aquaria.

It is important to realize before we get into a discussion of possible candidates for your nano display that many of the fish listed in this book have only recently come into the hobby. Many of them are from Southeast Asia, an area undergoing rapid development in terms of ornamental fish export. Fish from Burma, India, and Vietnam are all the rage, and almost every shipment has something new. The fact that you are reading this book indicates that you are the kind of aquarist who researches, and that's great. If you come across a likely species in your local store and it's not listed here, chase it down on the Internet. There's a good chance it's new, and a great many new fish are just perfect for nano setups. For now, though, let's take a look at many of the wonderful species already available.

A Note on Schooling

Many freshwater nano fish are schooling species. Schooling fish tend to be very skittish under the best of circumstances, and when kept alone or in pairs they actually will not thrive. The general rule for such fish is to keep at least six to eight as a minimum. For species suitable for nano tanks, it is probably better to consider ten to 12 the minimum size for a healthy school, as these tiny fish definitely feel safe only when in a sizable group. They look better in large groups, too.

Cypriniformes

As one of the most successful and numerous vertebrate orders, Cypriniformes has species with adult sizes ranging from less than an inch to more than a meter, and many are suitable for aquarium maintenance, with a good portion of them candidates for a nano setup. A small group is superbly suitable for nano systems. Let's look at some of these first.

Rasboras

New fish from Southeast Asia have excited many aquarists, and rasboras and danios are some of the hottest fish right now. Many new species have been introduced to the hobby recently, and some of them are excellent nano fish. The smaller danios can be considered, but the small rasboras are even better choices (see Figure 5.1).

While common names are never reliable, these small rasboras, many of which are new to the hobby, go by such a confusion of overlapping names that it is impossible to know what fish you are dealing with based on them. Fortunately, it doesn't matter that much, since they are all cared for the same way, and they all present similar displays in the aquarium. Rasboras are found principally in four genera.

Boraras

These diminutive fish are living jewels. Especially good candidates for a nano system, there are five described species in this genus:

- *Boraras brigittae* 35 mm (under 1½ inches)
- *Boraras maculatus* 25 mm (barely an inch)
- *Boraras merah* 20 mm (under an inch)
- *Boraras micros* 13 mm (half an inch)
- *Boraras urophthalmoides* 40 mm (just over 1½ inches)

The first three display brilliant red coloration and are especially beautiful against dark green plants. All are tiny schooling fish that will find most desktop aquaria extremely spacious. They are extremely peaceful, but because of their size they are in danger from all but the smallest tankmates. Some aquarists report difficulty in getting them to take prepared foods, and they certainly go wild for tiny live foods, but they can usually be coaxed into taking high-quality mini pellets or crushed flakes. Although they usually come from soft, acidic waters, they are quite adaptable.

Figure 5.1

Rasboras

Rasboras are fishes from four genera: *Boraras, Microrasbora, Rasbora* (all three featured here) and *Trigonostigma* (see Figure 5.3).

B. micros

Microrasbora erythromicron

Boraras brigittae

B. maculatus

M. nana

B. merah

B. urophthalmoides

M. rubescens

Rasbora agilis

R. brittani

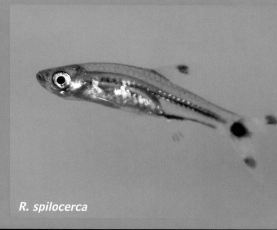

R. spilocerca

R. baliensis

R. meinkeni

R. borapetensis

R. rubrodorsalis

R. vaterifloris

Microrasbora

There is evidence that this genus is more closely related to the danios than the other three genera are. Most of the *Microrasbora* species are rather transparent, with subtle iridescent colors. The newly discovered (summer 2006) galaxy rasbora was tentatively considered to be in this genus but instead was placed into a new genus of its own. In any case, it has become one of the hottest fish of the new millennium! Like the *Boraras*, the fish in this genus are delightful little animals, and again there are five described species:

- *Microrasbora erythromicron* 20 mm ($^3/4$ inch)
- *Microrasbora gatesi* [no data available]
- *Microrasbora kubotai* 16 mm (just over $^1/2$ inch)
- *Microrasbora nana* 15 mm (just over $^1/2$ inch)
- *Microrasbora rubescens* 30 mm (an inch and a quarter)

Rasbora

There are many beautiful small species in this large genus (see Figure 5.2). There are a few large *Rasbora*, but most are well within our range for nano candidates. Some of perfect size are not listed here because they have never been brought into the hobby in any numbers, if at all. Hopefully they will be some day. It is worth researching any *Rasbora* you find available to see whether it will fit in a nano design. Many rasboras form schools that tend to hover in place, with the individual fish moving about within the school, but with the school moving rather slowly.

- *Rasbora agilis* 50 mm (2 inches)
- *Rasbora amplistriga* 34 mm (an inch and a third)
- *Rasbora baliensis* 35 mm (an inch and a third)
- *Rasbora beauforti* 20 mm (three-fourths of an inch)
- *Rasbora borapetensis* 40 mm (an inch and a half)
- *Rasbora brittani* 50 mm (2 inches)
- *Rasbora chrysotaenia* 35 mm (an inch and a third)
- *Rasbora dorsinotata* 43 mm (an inch and a half)
- *Rasbora johannae* 38 mm (an inch and a half)
- *Rasbora kalbarensis* 25 mm (1 inch)
- *Rasbora meinkeni* 39 mm (an inch and a half)
- *Rasbora paucisqualis* 40 mm (an inch and a half)
- *Rasbora rubrodorsalis* 33 mm (an inch and a third)

Figure 5.2

Rasbora spp.

While some *Rasbora* are too large for a nano setup, there are at least a dozen species that are small enough to consider.

Rasbora sp.

Rasbora borapetensis

Figure 5.3

Trigonostigma spp.

The new genus *Trigonostigma* contains the old favorite *T. heteromorpha* and a couple of similar but even more colorful new species.

Trigonostigma heteromorpha

T. hengeli

- *Rasbora sarawakensis* 38 mm (an inch and a half)
- *Rasbora spilocerca* 26 mm (1 inch)
- *Rasbora subtilis* 40 mm (an inch and a half)
- *Rasbora tuberculata* 27 mm (1 inch)
- *Rasbora vaterifloris* 40 mm (an inch and a half)

Trigonostigma

Four rasboras were transferred to this genus in a revision of the group in 1999. Three of these species are available in the hobby and are good candidates for a nano setup, with lengths of 25 to 50 mm (one to two inches). These include the "original" rasbora (see Figure 5.3) in the hobby, *Trigonostigma heteromorpha*, also known as the harlequin fish. All three of these rasboras are similar and sport a dark triangle marking on their sides. They are all found in the hobby, but the two smaller species—*T. espei* and *T. hengeli*—are a little harder to find. The fourth species, *T. somphongsi*, has a black stripe in place of the triangle, and it has yet to become established in the hobby.

In contrast to most cyprinids, these fish are not egg scatterers and instead spawn in pairs, placing eggs individually on the underside of leaves. They will eat their eggs and fry, but in a heavily planted tank you may well have some young survive.

Danios

As mentioned earlier, many danios are too active for most nano setups. However, the traditional distinction between rasboras, subfamily Rasboriniae, and danios, subfamily Danioninae, has become blurred with recent taxonomic findings. Many consider the genus *Microrasbora* to be danionine. The new genus *Celestichthys* is definitely a danio. This and many other recent discoveries (e.g., *Danionella*, *Sundadanio*) are small to tiny fish that could be great nano specimens. Once called rasboras, they can be considered for the most part to be small, less active danios. This group includes the genus *Paedocypris*, and *P. progenetica* is now recognized as the smallest known vertebrate, with an adult maximum size of 7.9 mm, hardly larger than an eyelash. This is truly a bizarre fish, living in peat swamps in Sumatra in water with a pH of 3—the same as vinegar! Its brain is not encased in skull bone, and the fish retains many larval features. Known only since 2005, this fish has not been imported and may very well be endangered, but were it in the hobby, it obviously would be a good candidate for a nano system!

Celestichthys margaritatus

Discovered in 2006, this species, first known as *Microrasbora* sp. "galaxy," was an instant hit. In spite of initial reports, this species is not endangered from overcollecting and remains viable in its native habitat. In any case, soon most specimens in the trade should be tank bred. A danio, not a rasbora, this fish likes to hide among aquatic vegetation and is an ideal candidate for a planted nano tank. This fish is a beautiful newcomer to the hobby. Maturing at 21 mm (three-quarters of an inch), it is a colorful and peaceful schooler that prefers hanging about in the plants to zipping around the tank like most of its danio relatives. It breeds readily, and in a well-planted tank some fry should survive. Or you can set up a breeding tank to maximize yield.

Barbs

Like danios and rasboras, barbs are for the most part schooling fish, but they tend to be chunky bodied, so for a nano tank they have to be quite small so that a group can be accommodated. In addition, barbs tend to be outgoing and a bit aggressive, though the

Celestichthys margaritatus is commonly known now as the celestial pearl danio.

Puntius titteya (left and right)

smallest species are not usually a problem. Most barbs available in the hobby are too large and too energetic for nano tanks. In fact, many species—such as the popular 14-inch (35-cm) tinfoil barb, *Barbonymus schwanenfeldii*—are too large and too energetic for many larger tanks! There are several species called "dwarf barbs," but at least one, *Puntius phutunio*, is too large for our purposes here at 80 mm (3 inches).

There are also species about 2 inches (5 cm) long that are a bit less active, like the cherry barb, *P. titteya*, which can go well in a tank of 10 gallons (40 liters) or more. One of the most beautiful possibilities is a tank with a lush growth of dark green Java moss and a school of these barbs. *P. gelius*, one of the species called the gold barb, is another possibility, but these fish are on the border of the nano concept.

P. gelius

There do exist in the hobby a few truly diminutive barb species, of which perhaps the most exciting import in recent years is the African *Barbus jae*, which is a beautiful reddish fish that attains only about 38 mm (an inch and a half). The largely transparent *Barboides gracilis* (see Figure 5.4) is an even smaller species from Africa, 18 mm (three-quarters of an inch). Both of these species show up regularly on importers' lists. An even smaller congener, *B. britzi,* was just described in 2006; this yellow barb should prove a great aquarium specimen if it ever becomes available.

Figure 5.4

Barbs and White Clouds

Barbus jae

Barboides gracilis

Tanichthys albonubes

T. micagemmae

White Clouds

For a very long time the white cloud mountain fish, *Tanichthys albonubes,* has been an aquarium favorite. Beautiful, colorful, peaceful, easy to breed, and hardy, these tiny subtropical Asian fish are perfectly happy at room temperature. Reports are that this species is extinct in the wild, but it is ubiquitous in the hobby. Domestic strains—longfin and gold morphs—are also well established. A second species, *T. micagemmae*, was described in 2001 and has become an instant hit in the hobby. It is sometimes called the blue white cloud (see Figure 5.4). A third species, *T. thacbaensis*, was also described in 2001, but it has not appeared in the trade yet.

Both aquarium species are ideal for nano setups, but you must remember to keep a school of them. The juveniles have an iridescent stripe that positively glows—it is more intense than that of the neon tetra, *Paracheirodon innesi*, and the adults remain very colorful, though the stripe loses some of its brilliance.

These fish generally do not bother their eggs or fry, so in a planted single-species tank you should soon have fish of all sizes. In community settings some fry may survive, but it depends on the type of cover provided and the nature of any tankmates.

Loaches

Most fish in the family Cobitidae, known as loaches, are way too large and energetic for a nano setup. Two notable exceptions come immediately to mind, however:

Pangio kuhlii, the kuhli loach, grows to about 12 cm (less than 5 inches), but it is extremely thin bodied, and it is not an active fish, spending most of its time hiding or crawling over the substrate slowly. Thus, it presents much less bioload than most fish of the same length, and a large group can be kept in a tank as small as 10 gallons (40 liters). They are extremely social and will pack themselves tightly into nooks and crannies. A true nocturnal species, they will nevertheless learn to come out at feeding time, when they pick up food from the substrate. They simply cannot compete for food, so any tankmates have to be very mild mannered.

Pangio kuhlii (left)
Yasuhikotakia sidthimunki (right)

A desktop aquarium stocked with a group of these and outfitted with a hunk of driftwood with a concave hollow on the base will often look like an unpopulated tank, but drop in some sinking food and the swarm of loaches will crawl out from under the wood to pick up tidbits from the gravel.

Yasuhikotakia sidthimunki is the smallest of the Botiinae (botia-like loaches), growing to 55 mm (just over 2 inches). Commonly called the dwarf loach, dwarf botia, dwarf chain loach, and Sid the monkey, this fish is not always available, and it can command a high price. Since you must have a school for them to thrive, it makes for an expensive setup, but well worth the price! Like the dwarf *Corydoras* catfish, this loach tends to spend time in mid water rather than on the bottom. Again, this is a species for the larger nano setups—10 gallons (40 liters) or more.

Characiformes

This large group is usually burdened by the misleading common name "characins," which should probably be restricted to the family Characidae but is often applied to any characiform fish as long as it is not very large. This order of fish is very well represented in the aquarium hobby. There are many small fish called tetras both in Central and South America and in Africa. The African species are not as common in the hobby as the popular South American tetras, but many are good candidates for nano systems if you can find them.

Critically Endangered

Yasuhikotakia sidthimunki populations once thrived in rivers in their native Thailand, but now their numbers are scarce as the result of environmental disruption. It is currently considered a critically endangered species, and this may be one popular aquarium fish that could very well become extinct in Nature.

Figure 5.5
African Tetras

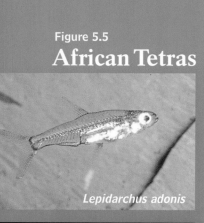
Lepidarchus adonis

Ladigesia roloffi

Neolebias ansorgii

N. powelli

African Tetras

The families Alestiidae and Citharinidae contain some very large predatory fish, but also a great many tiny species perfect for nano setups (see Figure 5.5). Especially appropriate are many *Neolebias* tetras, many of which attain lengths of only an inch or less. Some African tetras you may see include:

- *Lepidarchus adonis*: called the jelly bean tetra, a true miniature at about 27 mm (1 inch).
- *Ladigesia roloffi*: about 35 mm (less than an inch and a half) that is also often sold under the name jelly bean tetra. When in good condition and the right light, they positively glow.
- *Neolebias ansorgii* 26 mm (1 inch)
- *Neolebias axelrodi* 22 mm (just under an inch)
- *Neolebias powelli* 18 mm (three-quarters on an inch)
- *Neolebias trilineatus* 33 mm (an inch and a third)
- *Neolebias unifasciatus* 48 mm (under 2 inches)

American Tetras

The family Characidae has more than 1,000 species, from large piranhas to tiny tetras. As among the barbs, some of these tetras are more active than others, so you should not consider size alone when deciding on candidates for your setup. While many barbs and danios school by racing along together, many tetras flit about in schools that move slowly as a unit through the habitat, much like rasboras. There is considerable movement within the school, but the school itself meanders. The many small American tetras available (see Figure 5.6) include:

- *Hemigrammus bellottii* 26 mm (an inch)
- *Hyphessobrycon roseus* 20 mm (less than an inch)
- *Hyphessobrycon eques* complex 30 mm (just over an inch). The "serpae" tetras include a number of extremely similar species.
- *Hyphessobrycon flammeus,* 25 mm (an inch), the flame tetra
- *Paracheirodon simulans*, 20 mm (less than an inch), sometimes called the "false neon tetra"
- *Paracheirodon innesi*, 22 mm (about an inch), the neon tetra
- *Hemigrammus erythrozonus*, 33 mm (an inch and a third), the glowlight tetra
- *Hasemania nana,* 27 mm (about an inch), the silvertip tetra
- *Odontocharacidium aphanes*, 17 mm (just over half an inch), green dwarf tetra

Figure 5.6

American Tetras

Hemigrammus bellottii

Paracheirodon simulans

Hyphessobrycon roseus

Paracheirodon innesi

Odontocharacidium aphanes

Pristella maxillaris

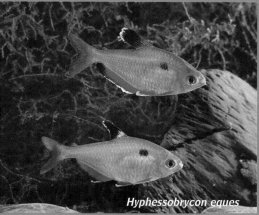
Hyphessobrycon eques

Hemigrammus erythrozonus

Aphyocharax paraguayensis

Hyphessobrycon flammeus

Hasemania nana

Axelrodia stigmatias

Hyphessobrycon eques

- *Nanocheirodon insignis* 24 mm (an inch)
- *Pristella maxillaris*, 45 mm (an inch and three-quarters), the X-ray tetra or pristella
- *Aphyocharax rathbuni*, 45 mm (an inch and three-quarters), green fire tetra or red flank bloodfin
- *Aphyocharax paraguayensis*, 35 mm (an inch and a half), the dawn tetra
- The genus *Axelrodia* comprises three or four species, all around 20 mm (less than an inch), and all good nano candidates.
- The genus *Brittanichthys* comprises two species, both around 30 mm (less than an inch and a half).

Other American Characiforms

The family Lebiasinidae contains splash tetras and pencilfish. There are a few large species, but most are very small. The actual splash tetra, *Copella arnoldi,* gets its name from its breeding behavior. In a series of carefully choreographed leaps, both the male and female jump from the water, landing vent-up on the underside of a leaf overhanging the water. Once this acrobatic spawning is completed, the male tends the eggs, splashing water up onto them periodically to keep them moist. When the fry hatch, they fall down into the water. This species and many of the similar species in the genus *Pyrrhulina* range from about 34 mm (an inch and a third) to about 70 mm (under 3 inches). All are attractively marked, and some are very colorful (see Figure 5.7). The pencilfish in the genus *Nannostomus* are great nano candidates. Many of the species are 30 mm (just over an inch) or less. At the time of this writing, the coral red pencilfish *N. mortenthaleri,* which was described in 2001, is extremely popular. This 29-mm (just over an inch) beauty is marked with dark red and black horizontal bands.

Nannostomus unifasciatus, just one of the species in this genus that make perfect nano specimens.

Figure 5.7

Characiforms

Copella arnoldi

Pyrrhulina sp.

Pyrrhulina sp.

Pyrrhulina laeta

Figure 5.8

Corydoradinae

Many species of small armored catfish are coming in with more regularity, and aquarists should have plenty of choices for catfish for nano setups, especially once they are successfully bred in captivity.

This 2.5-gallon (10-liter) planted tank, with a 9W compact fluorescent bulb for plant growth, was used to house baby *Corydoras* catfish.

Corydoras habrosus

C. pygmaeus

Aspidoras sp.

Aspidoras menezesi

Aspidoras sp.

A. pauciradiatus

A. virgulatus

79

Figure 5.9

Subfamily Hypoptopomatinae

Although they can be delicate when first imported, tiny "oto cats" make great additions to a nano display. They must be kept in groups, and they must be fed algae or equivalent foods.

Otocinclus vestitus

O. vittatus

un-*Corydoras*-like manner. They are all under an inch long and include *C. habrosus* at 20 mm, *C. hastatus* at 24 mm, and *C. pygmaeus* at 21 mm.

Also in this subfamily is the genus *Aspidoras*. These catfish are in many ways dwarf versions of cory cats. They are uncommon in the hobby, but are available from time to time. The various species range from 21 to 42 mm (less than an inch to an inch and a half) and thus are better suited for nano setups than their larger cousins (see Figure 5.8).

Hypoptopomatinae

Sucker-mouth catfish of the family Loricariidae, often called plecos, include many species that are quite large—2 feet (60 cm) or more. The family does include some petite species in the subfamily Hypoptopomatinae, genera *Otocinclus, Parotocinclus, Pseudotocinclus, Hisonotus*, and others (see Figure 5.9).

These "oto cats" are very popular with aquatic gardeners, since they remain small and eat algae. Wild-caught specimens are often loaded with parasites, and initial mortality can be very high. Once acclimated, however, they are hardy, peaceful animals.

There are several species of dwarf South American cats in the sole genus in the family Scoloplacidae: *Scoloplax*. They are all between 10 and 20 mm (less than a half inch to about three-quarters of an inch). Infrequently seen, these catfish would probably make good nano tank specimens if they became available in the hobby.

Madtoms

Among our native fish is a group of dwarf catfish in the genus *Noturus,* called madtoms, that can be used in unheated setups. Although no madtom species is very big, they average 10 to 15 cm (4 to 6 inches), a bit large for most nano tanks. A couple, however, are much more suitable for a nano setup: the pygmy madtom, *Noturus stanauli,* at 42 mm (an inch and a half) and *N. hildebrandi* at 69 mm (2 and 3/4 inches). The tadpole madtom, *N. gyrinus,* grows to about 120 mm (less than 5 inches), albeit slowly, and it comes from still waters, unlike most other madtoms, which prefer riffles and other areas of high water flow. This means that the tadpole madtom can adapt more easily to an aquarium without the need for the special powerheads that swift-water fish often require.

Madtoms are nocturnal and appreciate hiding places in the aquarium, but they quickly learn to come out for food during the day. That food can be just about anything, as they are typical catfish in accepting any food—prepared, frozen, freeze dried, or living. Although not specialized piscivores, they will, of course, consume any tankmate small enough to swallow whole.

Dwarf Sunfish

The genus *Elassoma* (see Figure 5.10) comprises a half dozen species most about 34 mm (less than an inch and a half) long, though *E. zonatum* reaches 47 mm (just under 2 inches). This genus is the only one in the family Elassomatidae, and their relationship to the sunfish of the family Centrarchidae is not clear and may be one of only superficial resemblance.

These fish inhabit swamps and are ideally suited for heavily planted desktop aquaria. An unheated tank is fine in most cases. Their major drawback is that they require live foods; most specimens simply cannot be weaned onto other types of food.

Labyrinth Fishes

The families of bettas, paradise fish, and gouramis have undergone and are still undergoing massive restructuring. For now, Osphronemidae includes almost all of them, from the 30-inch (750-mm) giant gourami, *Osphronemus goramy,* to the tiny *Parosphromenus* gouramis, many of which are less than 25 mm (1 inch). The habitat of many of these species includes stagnant swamps, bogs, and rice paddies, and they are adapted to these oxygen-poor environments by virtue of their labyrinth organ, which enables them to breathe atmospheric air. Also, since they typically live in shallow water among tangles of vegetation, they are not very active fish, and many of them are ambush predators who wait for their dinner to come to them. All of this means that these animals can be considered for nano setups at larger sizes than most other fish.

Often considered the first "tropical" fish, the paradise fish, *Macropodus opercularis,* is actually a subtropical species that will thrive at room temperatures and makes a much better subject for a typical betta bowl than the tropical *Betta splendens.* An albino strain is well established in the hobby. The only drawback is the paradise's size of up to 4 inches (100 mm). Of course, in a properly heated and filtered nano system, a male betta makes a great display, as would two or three female bettas, perhaps each of a different color. Other labyrinth genera to consider include:

Betta spp.

Aside from the popular *Betta splendens* there are many species often referred to as "wild bettas" (see Figure 5.11). It seems that every expedition to Southeast Asia brings back another new species or two. Most of these species are smaller than *B. splendens* (though there are some giants), and many are mouthbrooding species in which the male incubates the eggs in his mouth until they hatch and are free swimming. Since these fish

Figure 5.10

Dwarf Sunfish

The unique natives in the genus *Elassoma* are perfect nano candidates as long as you can supply them with live foods.

Elassoma okefenokee.

E. zonatum

are generally wild caught, they are often hard to wean onto prepared foods, and many require very soft, acidic water, at least for breeding. Many aquarists have also found them extremely sensitive to *Oodinium* infection.

On the other hand, betta fanciers abound, and the keeping and breeding secrets of these beautiful species are being revealed all the time. If you are interested in them and were thinking of working with some of them, you can consider using a decorative nano setup to house—and perhaps breed—them.

Sphaerichthys

The group of gouramis known popularly chocolate gouramis are small and beautiful, but they are notoriously difficult to acclimate and maintain, and even harder to breed. Like many of the bettas, they are mouthbrooding species. The largest species is the one normally seen and to which the name chocolate gourami was originally applied, *Sphaerichthys osphromenoides*, at about 60 mm (about 2 inches), with *S. acrostoma, S. selatanensis*, and *S. vaillanti* all about 40 cm (an inch and a half). Evidence suggests that these tiny fish are quite aggressive toward each other, and successful aquarists have found that keeping a large group is the best way to handle aggression. This would rule them out as nano inhabitants, but a single specimen could be part of a nano community.

Sphaerichthys osphromenoides

Figure 5.11

"Wild Bettas,"
Betta spp.

B. anabatoides

B. brownorum

B. edithae

B. balunga

B. burdigala

B. enisae

B. bellica

B. coccina

B. falx

Figure 5.11 (continued)

"Wild Bettas,"
Betta spp.

B. foerschi

B. macrostoma

B. picta

B. fusca

B. persephone

B. prima

B. imbellis

B. pi

B. pugnax

B. pulchra

B. simorum

B. taenia

B. rutilans

B. simplex

B. tussyae

B. schalleri

B. smaragdina

B. unimaculata

87

Figure 5.12

Trichopsis and *Parosphromenus*

Parosphromenus filamentosus

P. deissneri

Trichopsis schalleri

T. pumila

T. vittata

Trichopsis

The genus *Trichopsis* contains three species, of which the smallest and the most frequently seen is the pygmy or sparkling gourami *T. pumila*, which I discussed in the Preface. This is the most easily kept of the three, though all are suitable for nano tanks (see Figure 5.12).

Parasphaerichthys

There are two diminutive species in the genus *Parasphaerichthys*, and one, the eyespot gourami, *P. ocellatus*, is occasionally seen. It grows to about 40 mm (about an inch and a half). A recently (2002) described congener with interesting orange and black markings appears to reach only half that length. This would make a great nano candidate if it becomes available in the hobby.

Parosphromenus

This is a fairly large genus with about 20 species, several of which were described in 2005. There are two that have been in the hobby for some time, *Parosphromenus filamentosus* at 40 mm (an inch and a half) and *P. deissneri* at about 30 mm (an inch). Called spiketail or licorice gouramis, these tiny fish are great for nano displays (see Figure 5.12).

Dario dario (left)
Badis badis (right)

Badids

The family Badidae contains about a dozen species in two genera. All are small and difficult to get to eat nonliving foods. *Dario dario*, a beautiful red fish, appears to have been known to science for close to 200 years, though the taxonomy of these fish has been confusing, but it only got its current genus name and became a popular aquarium specimen in the last decade. Because they are more colorful, males are often shipped without females. Maximum size is less than an inch. Known as the scarlet badis, it is an excellent choice for a nano setup.

Badis badis and its congeners are all small but feisty fish from Asia. Their taxonomy is complicated, with populations that are considered by some to be subspecies and by others to be full species. The care of all types is the same. Identification is hampered in part by the extreme ability of these fish to change color, leading to one of their common names: chameleon fish. Males grow to 80 mm (about 3 inches), but females are smaller and less colorful. These fish require rocks, driftwood, and plants to hide among and to establish territories. Although related to the labyrinth fish, the badids behave much like dwarf cichlids. The males maintain territories around their home caves. After spawning the male protects the eggs and newly-hatched fry. These often overlooked fish should gain in popularity as nano tanks become more common.

Poeciliidae

Among the well known livebearers only guppies, *Poecilia reticulata,* and Endler's livebearers (sometimes identified as *P. wingei*) are reasonable candidates for a nano tank. Mollies and swordtails are too large, and while a pair of platies *Xiphophorus maculatus* can be kept in a 5-gallon (20-liter) tank, there is nothing particularly nano about such a setup.

Certain *Poeciliopsis* species are of similar size to guppies and Endlers or even smaller. Many are under 2 inches (5 cm)—though do your homework, as some species are as large as 5 inches (13 cm)! The genus *Micropoecilia*, as its name suggests, contains species of small livebearers. The largest aren't very big—*M. branneri* has 30-mm (just over an inch) males and 40-mm (inch-and-a-half) females, and *M. parae* and *M. picta* have 30-mm males and 50-mm (2-inch) females. Not surprisingly, *M. minima* is the dwarf of the group, with 16-mm (half-inch) males and 23-mm (less than an inch) females. These guppy-like fishes are found for the most part in South America and feature grey females and variably colored males.

The US-native *Heterandria formosa* is in fact an ideal nano fish. It is extremely

Figure 5.13

Poeciliidae

Endler's livebearer

Poecilia reticulata

Micropoecilia parae

Poecilia reticulata

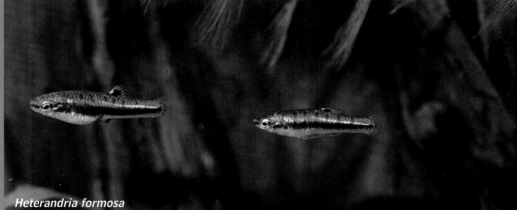

Heterandria formosa

Figure 5.14

Neolamprologus multifasciatus

A pair of *N.multifasciatus* near their shell.

N. multifasciatus in its shell.

A pair of *N. multifasciatus* with newly hatched fry.

attractive with its bold pattern, and as the smallest livebearing fish—and one of the smallest vertebrates—a colony can be observed in a very small aquarium without appearing crowded. The females are usually just one inch long (25 mm), and the males a little over half an inch (15 mm). Because of the female's size, she cannot hold a large brood of young, so instead the fry develop in a staggered fashion, with one or two completing development and being born each day until the entire litter has been born.

These fish eat absolutely anything from algae and live invertebrates to crushed flake food, but they do not pursue their relatively large offspring. They love a planted tank, and the thickets will soon hold fish of all ages. Because they are subtropical to temperate, in most cases a heater is not necessary, and room temperature will suit them fine (see figure 5.14).

Cichlidae

Cichlids may be the last thing you think of for a nano setup, but this incredibly diverse group truly has at least a species or two for any conceivable aquarium, from blackwater biotope to mini-reef, from indoor pond to nano tank. Once again, though, we want to distinguish between putting small fish into small tanks and setting up a nano system. Many breeders house pairs of *Apistogramma* in 5- to 10-gallon (20- to 40-liter) tanks, but a lot of fascinating behaviors are missed in such setups.

On the other hand, many of the Tanganyikan shell-dwelling cichlids live in aggregations of snail shells, and the fish rarely stray far from their homes. A group of these fish in the wild may never use much more space than they will have in a desktop aquarium and are therefore perfect candidates for a nano system. The fish live and breed inside their shells, and they are quite industrious when it comes to positioning their shells and grooming the substrate. Sometimes they will completely bury the shell, leaving only the opening exposed. Especially recommended are *Neolamprologus multifasciatus* (see Figure 5.14) and *Lamprologus ocellatus* (see Figure 5.15). Like all other Tanganyikan cichlids,

Figure 5.15

Lamprologus and *Mikrogeophagus*

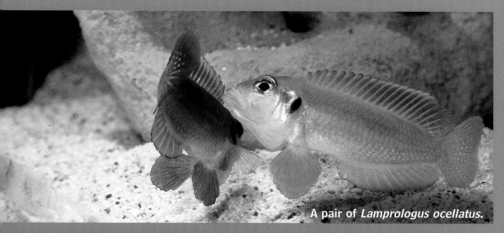

A pair of *Lamprologus ocellatus*.

L. ocellatus with juveniles.

Mikrogeophagus ramirezi

M. ramirezi, gold morph

M. ramirezi

M. ramirezi

these species insist on pristine water conditions, and the smaller the tank, the less buffer you have and the more persistent you must be with your water changes.

The *L. ocellatus* are best kept in harems, with one male and several females, each with its own shell. Even in very large aquaria a male will seldom tolerate the presence of another male. Multis are often kept in pairs, and one or two pairs could be your nano tank "colony." Some aquarists, however, have found these cichlids to be more productive when kept in harems as well.

Another option would be a pair of *Mikrogeophagus ramirezi* (see Figure 5.15). Known as rams or butterfly cichlids, these dwarf cichlids are ideal for nano tanks, not only because of their size—less than an inch and a half (about 3.5 cm)—but also because of their mild habits. You can keep a pair in a desktop tank of at least 5 gallons (20 liters). Not prodigious diggers, these cichlids are unlikely to decimate a planted tank, and provided they have a small clear area with a flat stone on which to deposit their eggs, they are likely to spawn and raise a batch of fry, providing you with all of the excitement and fascination of watching this complex parental behavior…but on a nano scale.

Another reason to consider a nano setup for these fish is that they are usually kept far too cold. They are a heat-loving species, best maintained at 81° to 86°F (27° to 30°C). Most aquaria are not kept that warm, so most rams are chilled. Having a small system just for these heat-loving cichlids can be an ideal solution.

Indostomus paradoxus

Asian Sticklebacks

The genus *Indostomus* contains three species that reach 25 to 30 mm (about an inch). Though uncommon in the hobby, they have recently started appearing on Asian exporters' lists. These are relatives of non-tropical sticklebacks, and all are related to seahorses and pipefish. Not much is known about aquarium care of *Indostomus*, but they certainly are of a size to consider a nano system.

Killies

The stereotype of a killifish breeder with a room full of tiny tanks—or maybe just plastic shoe boxes—each holding a bowl of peat moss and a pair of fish has some basis in fact. Most killie species are small, quasi-sedentary, and very attractive. In other words, they're perfect for nano setups. The non-decorative nature of most killie tanks is quite common in breeding setups of all kinds, but it is hardly necessary, and killies will do very well in beautifully aquascaped desktop aquaria. They are available in such a variety of form and color that you could easily populate a houseful of desktop, countertop, and bookshelf tanks with just killies of different species.

Although many killie specialists frown on keeping killies with other small fish such as tetras and livebearers, most killifish will do very well in a community setting. The main reason for aquarists' emphasis on maintaining killifish in individual breeding setups is that the fish are generally short lived, and they only breed for a short span of time; if you miss that window, your strain will die out. This does not mean, however, that if your focus is decorative you cannot make use of the gorgeous colors and finnage of killifish in nano tanks. And, while the bare utilitarian look is normal for a fishroom, it is possible to maintain many killie species in breeding colonies in planted ornamental aquaria, as often with heavy plant cover fry will survive, resulting in a tank full of fish of all sizes. European killifish hobbyists often favor this approach, which is ideal for nano applications.

Another factor that has kept killies a marginal specialty is the insistence of many of them on live foods. Some killifish fail to recognize anything that is not moving as food. It is not that difficult to culture live foods, however, and sometimes fussy killies will eat frozen food. Some killie species will even eat flake foods!

In general, fish in the genus *Aphyosemion* are the most suitable as beginner species (see Figure 5.16), though there are suitable fish in other genera. Killifish are a very diverse group, found in North and South America, Africa, Europe, and Asia. We could go through a long list of species and indicate which are most likely to adapt to a typical diet as well as live peacefully with their own fry. The problem is that this wouldn't help

Figure 5.16

Killifish, *Aphyosemion* spp.

A. ahli

A. calliurum

A. hera

A. australe

A. cameronense

A. primigenium

A. bualanum

A. caudofasciatum

A. striatum

Figure 5.17

Blue- and Lampeyes

Procatopus aberrans

Procatopus similis

Procatopus nototaenia

Pseudomugil sp.

Pseudomugil cyanodorsalis

Pseudomugil furcatus

Pseudomugil novaeguineae

Oryzias latipes

you much, since killies are not normally available in retail stores. This means that to acquire them you will have to contact a local breeder. That person can help you select the best choices for your nano killifish setup from the few species he or she raises. You can also observe them feeding and decide whether you will be able to maintain them on the foods you want to use. So how do you find a local killie breeder? Try a local aquarium society, retail store, or the American Killifish Association at www.aka.org.

Similar to killies, and often kept by killie specialists, are ricefishes such as *Oryzias latipes* and blue-eyes of the genus *Pseudomugil*, as well as the lampeyes, genus *Procatopus*. Most of these fish are between 30 and 50 mm (1 and 2 inches) (see Figure 5.17).

Puffers

There are a couple of species of freshwater puffers that can be considered for nano tanks by size, as several true freshwater species are in the 50- to 75-mm (2- to 3-inch) range, but their inquisitiveness and aggressiveness make small tanks problematic. The prime nano puffer candidate has to be *Carinotetraodon travancoricus*. This dwarf puffer barely makes 25 mm (1 inch) and is often called the pea or pygmy puffer.

As with all other puffers, these fish can be rather nippy, but their small size certainly limits the extent of their aggression. You can keep several together as long as the tank is aquascaped in such a way as to provide a multitude of hiding places and plenty of breaks in the line of sight. Some people are successful keeping them in large groups to diffuse the aggression. They have been successfully bred in captivity and like to place their eggs in a tangle of Java moss.

Puffers of all sizes are hunters, constantly prowling their territory to find prey. Wild-caught specimens may require live and frozen foods, while tank-bred fish will probably accept any and all foods you offer. A favorite of all puffers is live snails, but obviously this species can only handle the smallest snails.

Other Vertebrates

There are a few fully aquatic vertebrates other than fish you can consider for a nano aquarium. These do *not* include reptiles—no turtle is an animal for a nano tank, as even the tiniest turtles require more room and greater filtration than a desktop system can provide. A few amphibians, however, make good candidates.

Carinotetraodon travancoricus is truly a freshwater species, and you should not add salt to its aquarium, no matter what advice you receive.

Frogs

Two types of fully aquatic frogs are commonly sold for aquaria: the dwarf frogs of the genus *Hymenochirus* and the very large *Xenopus laevis*. The former is ideal for many nano systems, but *Xenopus* are too large, even for a single specimen display in most cases, and their voracious appetites and enormous mouths make them a danger in most large aquaria as well. The small juveniles usually available give little indication of the softball-sized adults they will become. They will eat anything they can fit into their mouths, and they use their arms to push the food down in. They will not hesitate to eat other frogs, including conspecifics smaller than themselves. An albino form is often offered as well as the dark wild type. They are fascinating animals, but they need large tanks.

The dwarf frogs barely reach 40 mm (an inch and a half). Their existence in the typical community aquarium is often marginal, as they can be attacked by larger fish, and they may not be able to compete successfully with them for food. In a nano tank, however, they will fare much better, and while they might eat a small rasbora if they were able to catch it, otherwise they are extremely peaceful, including toward each other. The only concern with desktop setups is that filtration has to be substantial, as these are messy animals. Of course, they are very small messy animals, and a rigorous water change regimen can make a smaller-than-normal aquarium adequate for the frogs.

Hymenochirus sp. This frog is a perfect fit for nano aquaria.

Some aquarists have been successful getting them to eat flakes or pellets, but usually they require small meaty foods, preferably live. These amphibians have been bred in captivity, but not regularly, and the tadpoles are tiny and difficult to raise.

Salamanders and Newts

Aquatic salamanders are another possible nano tank inhabitant. Almost all salamanders have aquatic larvae, some—the newts—have aquatic adult phases as well, and a few are neotonous, retaining gills and remaining aquatic throughout their lives. Many species are too large to consider here, but the larvae of small terrestrial salamanders, which can be collected in ponds and streams, are good candidates, as are the smaller newts like the native *Notophthalmus* species (see Figure 5.18) which are often offered for sale. Asian fire-bellied newts of the genus *Cynops* (see Figure 5.19) are also popular and inexpensive. These animals are dark on top, but their bellies range from orange to fiery red.

Newts present two problems as nano tank inhabitants. First is their propensity for escape. They can climb air tubing and wires, and they can even scale aquarium glass or climb up silicone seams. The aquarium, therefore, must be extremely securely covered. A wire screen top, with wires and tubing passing through small holes, is excellent. The animals need a place to haul out of the water, however, so you must provide floating plants or some sort of above-water platform, as well as sufficient airspace.

Feeding newts can be a challenge, as they often fail to recognize nonliving foods. Frozen foods like bloodworms and brine shrimp are the most likely to stimulate them to feed, but some specimens will readily take pellets. Flakes will probably be ignored. Blackworms or small earthworms are particular favorites.

Newts will not bother any fish or invertebrates too small to ingest and are generally peaceful with conspecifics, though there are exceptions, and it is never wise to combine different newt species.

Caecilians

The caecilians are an unusual group of tropical legless amphibians. They are the only amphibians that have scales. Most are terrestrial and burrowing, looking like snakes or large worms. A few species are aquatic, and *Typhlonectes natans* (see Figure 5.20) is regularly available in the trade under names like rubber worm, rubber eel, and Sicilian worm, the latter name undoubtedly based on a misinterpretation of "caecilian," as other than pronunciation, these animals have nothing to do with Sicily. As fascinating as these animals are, they are too large for a nano setup, since they reach lengths in excess of 870 mm (22 inches). There is, however, one way in which a caecilian could figure into a desktop display: a newborn caecilian.

Most if not all of the caecilians born in captivity are from females captured while pregnant that later give birth in someone's aquarium. If you had such an event occur in your tanks, you could temporarily house one or more of the babies in a nano system. With a soft sand substrate for burrowing and a cave or two to hide in, a caecilian display would work very well. It would not be long before the animal would have to be moved

Figure 5.18

Notophthalmus spp.

Notophthalmus viridescens (land form)

Notophthalmus sp.

N. viridescens (aquatic form)

Figure 5.19

Cynops spp.

Cynops orientalis

Cynops sp.

Cynops sp.

to larger quarters, but a desktop display would enable a much closer observation and appreciation of these fascinating nocturnal burrowing animals.

Nano Gardens

In many ways the planted aquarium is the freshwater equivalent of the reef tank. Both do not focus on fish, but instead on sessile photosynthetic organisms. Both require intense full-spectrum lighting, and both use complex testing and equipment to maintain the proper water chemistry, especially in terms of the nutrients needed by the photosynthetic organisms. The concept of *control* is very important to aquarists keeping either type of system. The nano aquatic garden shares many of the advantages and disadvantages of the nano reef, and as with a reef, the required control is more precise the smaller the aquarium gets. Since shallow freshwater habitats are not as stable as coral reefs, a planted nano is a bit less sensitive to temperature fluctuation, though it is still a real concern.

Diversity

Nevertheless, a nano system provides special options to the aquatic gardener. The tiniest of plants that are viewed as driftwood coverings or lawns in large tanks can be focused on in a nano. Plants that require water conditions vastly different from your water supply can be kept, since only a small volume of water needs to be prepared and maintained. The miniature versions of high-output lighting are comparably less expensive than the large versions, and the cost of running the lights is more reasonable, making a nano garden with high-light species much more affordable. If you want to experiment with different substrates, lighting, or fertilizing, it is far less trouble and expense to set up several nano tanks, or a succession of them, than to use large aquaria.

We've already mentioned keeping to the bonsai principle when planting a nano system (Chapter 3). The nano tank should focus

Figure 5.20

Typphlonectes sp.

Typhlonectes

Although they have no legs and look like eels, caecilians are amphibians. Only newborn caecilians could be considered for a nano tank, but such a display would provide a perfect opportunity to study an otherwise hard-to-observe animal.

Typhlonectes natans

8-Gallon (32-Liter) Planted Nano Tank

Attached to wood: *Taxiphyllum barbieri* (*Vesicularia dubyana*)
Foreground plant: *Elatine triandra*
Background, right side: *Lagarosiphon madagascariensis*
Background, middle: *Ludwigia brevipes*

A planted tank focuses on the pants, regardless of its size. All other organisms, whether vertebrate or invertebrate, come second. Fish and freshwater shrimp can be kept in nano garden, but specimens are kept sparingly.

on plants, putting a spotlight on specimens that would be noticeable only *en masse* in a regular aquarium. Java moss, which is typically used as an accent in a planted tank, can be not only the only plant in a nano, but also the central aquascaping feature. A single broad-leaf *Anubias* or *Cryptocoryne* plant—typically foreground plants—can be the centerpiece in a nano tank the way a large Amazon sword *Echinodorus* sp. is in a large aquarium.

Nano Lighting

Because the depth of a nano tank is typically much shorter than in most other setups, the plants are never far from the lights. This means that you can grow species that require intense light without using expensive and high-heat-producing lamps like metal halides. Fluorescent lights and a homemade yeast-based carbon dioxide system can produce luxuriant growth of species like *Glossostigma* that normally require much more

20-Gallon (80-Liter) Planted Nano Tank

Plants
Ludwigia arcuata, Rotala sp. "green," Eleocharis vivipara, Glossostigma sp., Micranthemum micranthemoides, Anubias nana
Livestock
Paracheirodon simulans, Rasbora maculata

2-Gallon (8-Liter) Planted Nano Tank

Plants
Hemianthus callitrichoides "Cuba"
Taxiphyllum barbieri (*Vesicularia dubyana*)
Riccia fluitans
Rotala sp. "Nanjenshan" (*Mayaca sellowiana*)
Eleocharis acicularis

Substrate
10 mm of fertilizer, 30 mm of pea gravel, hand-collected rocks from the south of England

Dimensions
8 x 8 x 8 inches (20 x 20 x 20 cm)

Lighting
20W halogen spot lamp, on 6 hours a day

Water Changes
50 percent every third day with dechlorinated tap water

Carbon Dioxide
One bubble per second through a glass diffuser for a total of 30 ppm during lights on

Anubias frazeri

expensive equipment to do well. The same is true for deep red plants that can be very tough to grow in aquaria of greater depth.

On the other hand, you can position a metal halide fixture—perhaps over a whole bank of nano tanks—with considerable room between the lamp and the water surface and still have intense enough light for hard-to-grow plants. This extra air space eliminates much of the overheating concern with these lights, making them a bit more practical for tanks with small water volumes.

The latest LED light systems hold great promise for nano systems. Their high light and low heat output makes them very attractive, as does their adaptability—they can be configured to produce very specific wavelengths and focused very tightly. Just really coming into their own, these lights should soon be available in a great many configurations.

Special Considerations

In some ways, nano aquatic gardens require less specialization that nano fish tanks. Plant growth and health is much less dependent on space; in almost all cases a vessel large enough to contain the mature plant is sufficient, while there are many fish that would fit into a tiny aquarium but not survive or thrive in it. In addition, it is common practice to prune aquatic plants as they grow—something with no piscine equivalent.

Thus, the husbandry of plants in nano tanks is extremely similar to that of plants in regular tanks. The main difference is in the selection of species and how they are used. The small volumes make it much easier to provide the proper water and lighting conditions, but those conditions are essentially the same in any aquarium. This contrasts, of course, with the husbandry of animals in nano tanks, since that must take into account all sorts of physiological and behavioral factors.

Cryptocoryne pontederifolia

For this reason, any planted tank resource is almost entirely applicable to nano systems, with the exception of advice about plant placement—foreground, background, centerpiece, etc. That is why this book does not go into detail about keeping plants in nano setups but concentrates on fish and invertebrates.

Specimen Display

There are a great many species of freshwater fish that can be used in a single-specimen or single-species setup. We've already mentioned many species that can be kept as breeding colonies in a planted nano tank. Ideal for a single display would be an interesting fish that does not do well with tankmates.

This 8-gallon (32-liter) garden aquarium showcases *Taxiphyllum barbieri* (*Vesicularia dubyana*) and a freshwater snail.

One unlikely candidate for a larger nano would be *Gobioides broussonnetii*. Known as the violet or dragon goby, this purplish eel-like fish grows to about 550 mm (22 inches). It can be found, and kept, in fresh, brackish, or full-marine water; it is probably best to maintain brackish conditions for it. The reason such a large fish could be considered for a nano setup is that besides being extremely elongate and totaling much less biomass than most other two-foot fish, this fish is sedentary.

A 10-gallon (40-liter) tank could house a single fish until it was half to two-thirds grown, provided you kept up with rigorous water changes. Despite its formidable appearance, this is a meek fish. All it wants is to lie in the mud and filter bits of food from the water and from the substrate. It cannot compete with tankmates and prefers a solitary existence. Provided with its own tank, a good hiding cave, soft substrate, and plenty of tiny food organisms, this fish that usually suffers being dumped into a community aquarium will instead thrive and provide a fascinating display.

Community Display

Many of the fish discussed in this chapter can be combined into interesting communities. When stocking a community aquarium of any size you should consider including bottom, midwater, and upper level species. This not only provides more interest but also minimizes competition and helps ensure peaceful coexistence. You must, however, resist the temptation to include a great variety of colorful species when they are schooling fish. Due to the stocking limitations of a nano system, you may often find that only a single school can be kept, meaning that many more "communities" will be species tanks than is true for larger setups.

Gobioides broussonnetii, a large
but sedentary fish.

Biotope Display

Whether you are interested simply in grouping fish and plants from one continent or
in re-creating a particular stream somewhere in the tropics, the species available in the
hobby today provide you with many possibilities. A nano setup can provide a very tight
focus on a biotope, perhaps illustrating a community of organisms living among the
leaves and roots of a single plant. By combining tiny fish with tiny invertebrates (see
next chapter) you can create a biotope focus of animals that would scarcely be noticed
in a regular community tank.

Freshwater Invertebrates

Chapter **6**

For a long time the only freshwater invertebrates common in aquaria were snails, and they were often unwelcome pests. Today aquatic invertebrates have come into their own, and some hobbyists maintain tanks just for inverts. Not all freshwater invertebrates are suitable for inclusion in a nano tank, but many are more than just suitable—they are perfect for such a setup. In this chapter we will look at the most popular species and groups, along with a few less usual candidates.

Crustaceans

Although this subphylum of Arthropoda has a few terrestrial species (pill bugs and wood lice) and a very small number of sessile forms (barnacles), the vast majority of crustaceans are motile aquatic invertebrates. Most of the 55,000 species are marine, but

A freshwater shrimp.

On Molting

Shrimp, crabs, and crayfish molt. The animal will become dull, and even its eyes will cloud over. Its shell then splits, and it climbs out, clad in a brand-new shell that is soft and flexible. All crustaceans molt, but growing juveniles molt much more often, since their rigid shells do not permit growth. While the shell is soft the animal pumps water into its body to expand it; when the shell solidifies, there will be a little extra space into which the animal can grow. Until the shell hardens the crustacean is vulnerable, and it must have a place to hide safely until it is again protected. The shed shell looks a great deal like a dead animal, and you should not be fooled into thinking your pet has expired when you find a shedding. Sometimes the animal will consume part or all of the cast-off shell.

Figure 6.1

Freshwater Shrimp

that still leaves plenty of freshwater species, many of which are diminutive enough to feature in a nano aquarium.

These creatures are omnivorous, and many are scavengers. A few are active predators, so the crustacean diet ranges from detritus to live fish, and the invertebrate should be carefully matched to its tankmates.

Shrimp

We have to start with shrimp, since they are the current stars of freshwater invertebrate tanks. The class Malacostraca includes the most commonly known crustaceans, and the name "shrimp" is applied to many species within this group, though not all are closely related. Marine, brackish, and freshwater species abound, and many have become established in the hobby in the last decade or two. Biologists distinguish between shrimp, suborder Pleocyemata, and the superficially similar prawns, suborder Dendrobrachiata, but those common names are applied indiscriminately in the trade and the hobby, often based on regional or culinary tradition, and as with all common names they should not be used for identification purposes.

Although freshwater shrimp (see Figure 6.1) were originally kept mainly as adjuncts to a planted aquarium, their beauty and behaviors have led many aquarists to give them tanks of their own. Once people started doing that, many were successful breeding the shrimp and soon wound up with tanks full of them. There is now a hefty trade in these animals, mostly from hobbyist to hobbyist. They have become aquarium subjects in their own right, and a nano setup is the ideal way to display and observe them.

Algae-Eating Shrimp

The genera *Caridina* and *Neocaridina* in the family Atyidae have garnered a spotlight thanks to Takashi Amano, the internationally famous aquatic gardener who popularized the use of these small shrimp to combat algae in planted tanks. In fact,

Caridinia japonica

Caridina japonica is often called the "Amano shrimp." Some species have a brackish or marine stage in their life cycle, while others can be propagated completely in fresh water. You will find these animals for sale under a huge variety of names, usually dependent on color or color pattern, such as crystal red shrimp, bumblebee shrimp, blue shrimp, cherry red shrimp, green shrimp, zebra shrimp, etc.

The taxonomy of these crustaceans is confusing, and identifying to the species level outside a laboratory is not always possible. In addition, many of the color forms available are domesticated strains that are not found (or are not commonly found) in wild populations. For example, the cherry red and blue shrimps are considered to be the same species, as are the crystal red and bumblebee shrimps. I say "considered to be" because these common names are flung around with little scientific concern. Some aquarists use "crystal red" and "cherry red" for the same species, while other assign them to two different species. Fortunately, an exact identification is not required to provide the proper care. Just keep only one variety per tank to avoid interbreeding. This is true for different color phases as well as different species.

These shrimp are scavengers and algae eaters and will do a very good job of cleaning up a tank, though aquatic gardeners often find them reluctant to harvest algae when there is plenty of easy-to-obtain fish food available. When kept in an aquarium of their own, they will eat just about any type of food you offer—flakes, pellets, frozen, algae wafers, etc.

The freshwater species have direct development, with no larval stage. The female carries her eggs under her tail until they hatch into miniature versions of the adult shrimp. In an aquarium without fish some of the young should survive, but make sure there are no filter strainers with spacing large enough to permit the tiny shrimp to be sucked in. You can wrap polyester filter material around the strainer and secure it with rubber bands to protect the shrimp—or even better, use a sponge filter, which will provide an additional food source with the microorganisms that flourish in the sponge.

In order to raise these shrimp intensively, maximizing the yield, it is necessary to move the newly hatched babies to accommodations of their own and feed them with various live food cultures. Daily water changes are required with this approach to maintain water quality. A mature tank with a big clump of Java moss and without predatory fish, however, will see the shrimp population increase without any special care. The juveniles feed off microorganisms in the aquarium until they are large enough to handle bits of the regular food.

Filter-Feeding Shrimp

The subfamily Atyinae contains *Caridina* and *Neocaridina*, the shrimp we just discussed, plus various filter-feeding species of the genera *Atya, Atyoida, Atyopsis,* and

Atya sp. (left)
Atyopsis sp. (right)

Palaemonetes sp.

others, called by names such as wood shrimp, fan shrimp, bamboo shrimp, vampire shrimp, etc. Their front claws are modified into pompoms that they wave back and forth, straining tiny particles from the water. They then bring them to their mouth to ingest the food.

These shrimp are not obligatory planktonivores, which would make them problematic for maintenance in an aquarium of any size. A more natural diet would be baby brine shrimp, cyclops, and the like, but they are also able to manipulate larger pieces of food into their mouths with their brushy feet, so they usually do quite well on the scraps from regular aquarium fare—crushed flake foods, for example.

Ghost Shrimp

Shrimp of the genus *Palaemonetes* are commonly called grass, glass, or ghost shrimp. These are small transparent shrimp, generally about an inch long. There are freshwater,

Figure 6.2
Long-Arm Shrimp

Macrobrachium rosenbergii

Macrobrachium sp.

Macrobrachium sp.

brackish, and marine species. The freshwater forms are widely available, mainly for use as live food for larger fish, but they are interesting in their own right and easy to keep. A planted tank suits them fine, and since as with all other crustaceans they are escape artists, they require a complete cover on the tank. They will eat just about anything, and because of their transparency you can see whatever they eat in their gut. They breed readily in captivity. The females carry the eggs under their abdomen until they hatch. Like other freshwater crustaceans, the freshwater species have direct development, which means the babies do not have a larval stage and are miniature versions of the adult when they hatch.

Long-Arm Shrimp

These shrimp are in the same family, Palaemonidae, as grass shrimp. The genus *Macrobrachium* (see Figure 6.2) is widespread in the wild but is not well represented in the trade. Macros have elongated arms and claws, making them a bit like crayfish in that regard. They also tend to be much more territorial and aggressive than most of the other species popular in the hobby. Many require brackish or marine water for successful reproduction, and the larvae require plankton. Most are fairly large, but there are a few smaller species that are available from time to time and could be considered for a nano display. In most cases a macro shrimp should be the only animal in the aquarium.

Scuds

Freshwater amphipods in the family Gammaridae often go by the common names "gammarus" and "scuds," though not all scuds are in the genus *Gammarus*. Those found in the trade in live food cultures are usually *Gammarus* or *Hyella* spp. The vast majority of scuds kept by aquarists are reared to feed fish, but these little laterally compressed "shrimp" can make a fascinating nano display. Their locomotion is particularly interesting. Most of the time they crawl through leaf litter or detritus on the bottom, but they will periodically make forays out into the water and even to the surface. They swim in bursts, a rapid acceleration followed by a short rest period during which they drift, then another burst. Their cryptic habits and small size invite extremely close and careful scrutiny— that important factor in the nano concept.

Obviously they cannot be kept with animals large enough to eat them, but otherwise they mix well with small invertebrates and fishes. They are effective scavengers and will clean up bits of food overlooked by their tankmates.

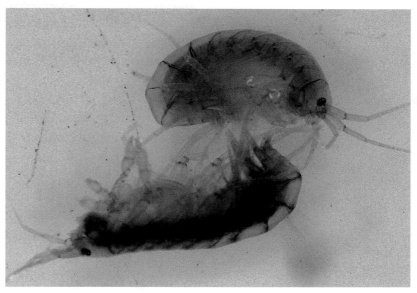

Gammarus sp.

Crayfish

Known as crayfish, crawfish, crawdads, mudbugs, freshwater lobsters, yabbies, and many other names, there are many species, often with captive-bred color morphs. Crayfish range from mildly cannibalistic to downright savage toward each other, so one per tank is the safest formula. Despite their long-term popularity among aquarists, crayfish are best not kept with fish. None will pass up the opportunity to eat a fish that swims too close, and some are quite adept at catching fish. In addition, all crayfish have to molt periodically, after which their shells are soft, and fish can pick them apart. They are also very vulnerable at this time to predation by any crayfish tankmates as well. Nevertheless, small enough crayfish and small enough fish can combine successfully, which means that crayfish can be candidates for a nano setup, either by themselves or with fish.

Female crayfish carry their eggs under their tails, and the babies hatch as miniature versions of the adult. Thus even the largest species are tiny as juveniles, and small crayfish of any kind can be used in nano systems and then moved to other quarters as they grow. There are also dwarf species that can be kept long term and bred in nano tanks, such as the increasingly popular *Cambarellus schufeldtii*.

The crayfish craze began in Europe and is now taking hold in the United States. A few species of crayfish show up regularly at aquarium stores, and many more are available

from specialist hobbyists, sometimes at steep prices. It may be possible for you to collect your own, however. Check local laws before setting out, and make sure you comply with all regulations. Stream crayfish are easily harvested. Position a net on the downstream side of a flat rock, then lift the rock. When the silt settles, you may have a cray or two in the net. A baited minnow trap can harvest pond dwellers.

Crayfish often live in mud burrows and can live for long periods out of the water as long as they are moist and can keep their gills wet. This adaptation enables them to be sent cross country in a box of moist sphagnum moss. It also enables them to survive levels of ammonia pollution that would otherwise burn off their gills, and it is common to find large crayfish kept in small containers with about an inch of water and a rock or branch onto which they can climb to get out of the water. Such a setup is workable for a nano display, but fill the same container with water and the crayfish will quickly die. So if you want a fully aquatic display, stick to tiny specimens and make sure you have a good biofilter.

Crabs

Truly freshwater crabs are not too common, but there are some, and several brackish species will tolerate fresh water for prolonged periods. More of a concern is the fact that many species need a place where they can get completely out of the water. It is not uncommon to find even marine species that inhabit tidepools and beaches, but many freshwater crabs seem more to be terrestrial species that take a dip occasionally. To make things more difficult, it can be very hard to find properly identified crabs for sale, or to identify them as to species using reference texts and keys. Unless you know for sure that a crab is a totally aquatic freshwater species, it is best to provide it with a perch above the water line—perhaps with a piece of driftwood that juts out of the water.

Crabs are typically scavenging omnivores, often sifting through detritus for edible tidbits. Most will take any aquarium fare, but remember they may need to be fed out of the water. Almost any crab will catch and kill small prey as well, so be careful to match claw size against potential tankmates.

Vernal Pond "Shrimp"

Vernal ponds are temporary bodies of water, ranging from mere puddles to sizable ponds. They are often found in arid areas and are completely dependent on rainfall for their existence. Others are found in rainforests and appear during the rainy season but dry up in the dry season. In dry years they may not form at all. Animals that exploit

Fiddlers

Fiddler crabs are often available in the hobby and sold as freshwater aquatics. The genus *Uca* contains many similar species, most brackish or marine. All of them inhabit beaches or tidal mudflats and spend considerable time foraging and waving their big "fiddle" claws at each other on land during low tide. Some aquarists are successful in keeping them long term in freshwater aquaria, but the ideal setup for them is part water, part sandy shore.

Uca sp.

Uca sp.

Uca minax

123

Land hermit crabs only need a small bowl of water. Anything larger and the crab may drown in it.

these habitats must be able to perpetuate their species even during drought. For many this entails the production of dormant eggs or cysts that can survive being dried in a state of diapause. In some cases it is more than a year before sufficient rains return, and the eggs can often survive a decade or more and still hatch out when rehydrated.

Fish are extremely rare in these biotopes, being restricted to a few annual killifish species in tropical rainforests, so invertebrates are the major inhabitants of vernal ponds. Amphibian larvae are also common, as some frogs and salamanders have adapted to this environment with extremely rapid growth and maturation to get the juveniles through metamorphosis before the pond dries up. Speed is also the theme for invertebrates, which often can complete a life cycle in two weeks.

Fairy Shrimp

The freshwater counterpart of brine shrimp, the crustacean best known to aquarists as food for fish, fairy shrimp of the class Branchiopoda can be found in a variety of habitats, often in vernal pools in arid areas. Most are small, about 10 mm (less than half an inch), but there are some large predatory species more than 150 mm (6 inches) long. These animals typically swim upside down, their legs to the surface, and they demonstrate graceful antics like those of brine shrimp that gave them the name "sea monkeys." Their color varies, being largely dependent on diet. They are not commercially available, but they are occasionally collected by aquarists, either to feed their fish or to be kept in a small tank by themselves. They are perfect for a nano setup, provided there is nothing in the tank large enough to eat them. The animals are very short-lived, but they will produce eggs that will hatch without being desiccated, so a continual colony is possible. If the culture ever fails, you can pour out the water and let the substrate dry completely, then refill the tank. With a little luck you will soon have a new population of shrimp from dormant eggs.

Triops cancriformis

Triops

These notostracans are truly ancient, virtually unchanged during the last couple hundred million years. In fact, *Triops cancriformis* is a good candidate for oldest animal

Fairy shrimp.

Figure 6.3

Snails

Pomacea bridgesii

Pomacea bridgesii

Ramshorn snail.

species, being apparently the same today as it was when it appeared 220 million years ago. Called tadpole or shield shrimp, from the top they look a bit like tiny horseshoe crabs *Limulus* spp. They will eat anything, including detritus, but they are extremely predatory and prefer to eat living animals, including each other. Their rapid life cycle has made them popular as pets and for school projects, and with a little luck several generations can be raised in succession. Tankmates are basically out of the question, since anything small enough not to eat the shrimp will be eaten by them.

Mollusks

The ironic phylum name Mollusca (from the Latin *mollis*, meaning "soft") was first used for cephalopods (e.g., octopus and squid). Later the relationship of these pliable animals to the more numerous hard-shelled gastropods (e.g., snails) and bivalves (e.g., clams) was discovered. There are no freshwater cephalopods, but the classes Gastropoda and Bivalvia (Pelecypoda) have many freshwater species, several of which figure prominently in the aquarium trade.

Snails

All aquarium snails are possible candidates for a nano setup, and whether you plan to include them or not, they may appear in your aquarium. Snails were kept in Victorian aquaria with the idea that they are part of the balance between plants and animals that keeps a small glass-enclosed ecosystem going. The balanced aquarium myth has faded, and although snails are still used by many fish breeders to consume leftover food in fry tanks, they spent a long time out of favor with most aquarists because of their prolific breeding habits and occasional appetite for live plants.

Recently their popularity has improved, especially for the ampullariid apple and mystery snails, which are available in an array of color morphs and most of which lay their eggs in masses above the water line, making it very easy to control their population. Correctly identifying these snails can be difficult. Generally mystery snails are considered to be *Pomacea bridgesii*, but there are several similar species that are commonly available (see Figure 6.3). Many of them are hardened plant eaters, while some species stick mostly to algae for their veggies. Unlike most other snails, which are hermaphroditic, individual apple snails are either male or female.

The largest snail in this group is a massive softball-sized handful, and the smallest is the attractively banded *Asolene spixi*, which tops out at 25 mm (an inch) and is often called the zebra apple snail. This snail may burrow into the substrate and is most active at night.

While ampullariid snails are often purchased, sold, and bred intentionally, common pond and ramshorn snails are more typically uninvited guests, arriving on aquatic plants. Pond snails are usually *Physa* spp., and there are a couple of genera and several species of ramshorn snails, which come in a few colors, including a rich mahogany red. These are the snails that multiply rapidly and can quickly overrun an aquarium. Generally they will not eat healthy plants. Some aquarists culture them to feed to cichlids, puffers, or loaches.

The Malaysian trumpet snail *Melanoides tuberculata* is a burrowing snail that remains buried during the day and comes out at night to scavenge for food. The cornucopia shell is long and narrow, tapering to a point, and about 25 mm (an inch) long. The shell is extremely hard, and many snail-eating fish cannot crack it. These snails do not harm plants and keep the substrate stirred with their digging, so they are popular with many planted tank enthusiasts.

Nerite snails of the genus *Nerites* have become very popular in recent years in the reef hobby because of their appetite for algae. These are adaptable snails that can often be acclimated from their native brackish water to fresh or full marine. It is likely that there are different species with different salinity tolerances, as a few aquarists have been successful reproducing these snails in fresh water, while in most cases the snails need brackish conditions to reproduce.

Many aquarists view snails as weeds, but a universal truth about gardening is that one person's weed is another's prize specimen. Even the much unappreciated pond snail is a fascinating creature, with unique locomotion and interesting behaviors. A nano aquarium provides the perfect setting for examining such an animal, and it forces us to step back and scrutinize something we were either taking for granted or plotting to eliminate.

A freshwater mussel.

Clams and Mussels

Filter-feeding bivalves are, in general, a poor choice for a nano aquarium. True, they tend to be small and don't need room to move around, and they are peaceful toward anything large enough to see with the naked eye, but the fact that they are filter-feeding bivalves itself indicates the problems in keeping them.

Filter feeders can feed only on microscopic food particles—usually plankton—and they need large quantities of them. A couple of mussels can clear a 5-gallon (20-liter) tank of a pea-soup algae infestation in a few hours; after which they will quickly starve unless offered some equivalent food source on a regular basis. And, since they are bivalves (two shells), they don't look too much different when they do die—of starvation or any other cause. Often the first indication of the demise of one of these creatures is the foul stench coming from the aquarium, which is by then toxically polluted.

On the other hand, if you have a steady supply of phytoplankton or some other food, and if you make it a habit to observe them closely and often, freshwater clams and mussels would make interesting specimens for a nano setup.

Insecta

The class Insecta is the most successful macroscopic animal group on Earth, with several million species found in just about every habitat, though only a minute minority are aquatic, with only a handful of those being marine species. On the other hand, many terrestrial insects have larvae that live in fresh water, and there are a few common insects with aquatic adult forms.

Aquarists are familiar with the larvae of chironomid midges, known as bloodworms and frequently fed to fish live, frozen, and freeze-dried, and aquatic mosquito larvae are also widely utilized as live food for aquarium fish. There are many species of insects besides these which can be considered for the aquarium.

Dragonfly Nymphs

Fish predators like dragonfly nymphs are also known to aquarists, who usually encounter them as contaminants in live food cultures or hiding in live aquatic plants. It is difficult to house them in an aquarium with fish, since it is hard to find a balance between fish large enough not to be eaten by the nymphs and small enough not to eat the nymphs.

On the other hand, these fascinating underwater dragons can make a spectacular display, either alone or with other aquatic insects, and they invite the kind of close scrutiny that is central to the nano concept. If you're lucky, you may even get one to pupate and hatch out as a beautiful dragonfly or darning needle.

Diving Beetles

The family Dystiscidae contains many species of beetles that are aquatic in all life stages. Both larvae and adults are predatory, so, again, it is tough to balance between fish prey and fish predators. It is also possible some of your bugs will chow down on others.

Dragonfly nymph, *Cordulegaster* sp.

Close-up of a sunburst diving beetle, *Thermonectus marmoratus*.

Then again, a tank stocked by netting insects in a local pond or swamp will be a dynamic and interesting display even if the population is constantly changing due to predation.

Sponges

The phylum Porifera has 5,000 species, of which only about 150 are freshwater. While marine sponges can be quite colorful, even beautiful, most freshwater forms are small and nondescript. They offer a challenge since they are filter feeders and require a steady supply of copious microorganisms as food. They are much more likely to survive in a large system that can generate food organisms than in a nano setup.

Cnidarians

The phylum Cnidaria is even larger than Porifera, with about 9,000 species but even fewer freshwater species—only a couple of dozen. Those few are known as hydra, and most aquarists, if they know them at all, know them as pests that proliferate in fry tanks and that can capture and eat the smallest of fish. These animals do deserve a second look, however, especially in terms of a nano system.

Hydra are certainly small—the largest barely make an inch (a couple of centimeters), and most are smaller—and they are fascinating. Though they do not actually swim, they can drift with the currents, and they can cover remarkable distances by somersaulting—bending down to bring their tentacles to the substrate, then releasing their stalk, bending it over and reattaching a body length away, then repeating the procedure. With their tentacles they sting small prey animals, then draw them to their mouth for ingestion. They come in a variety of colors, including green, which is a result of symbiotic algae that live within the hydra's tissues the same way zooxanthellae inhabit marine corals and anemone.

The reason these animals are such a pest in fry tanks is that they thrive on a diet of live baby brine shrimp. While an aquarium could have a few unnoticed hydra in it, a fry tank flooded regularly with brine shrimp can experience a cnidarian population explosion until they cover the glass and everything else in the tank. Even if they weren't a danger to small fry, their diet would represent a significant waste of carefully cultured shrimp. So be prepared for some odd looks from aquarists if you tell them you raise hydra on purpose.

Water Bears

The phylum Tardigrada, with about 750 extant species, is one of the most ancient, widespread, and successful groups of animals on the planet—and completely unknown to most people despite population densities in some habitats of 25,000 per liter (100,000 per gallon)! Water bears are found literally everywhere, from desert hot springs to polar ice, from vernal pools to deep ocean sediments, from patches of moss or lichens to slate roofs. These animals are able to undergo complete desiccation, freezing, baking, and irradiation in cryptobiosis—a state that makes hibernation look like strenuous activity. Why are they so unfamiliar? Their complete obscurity in size and

Freshwater hydra.

Marine Fishes

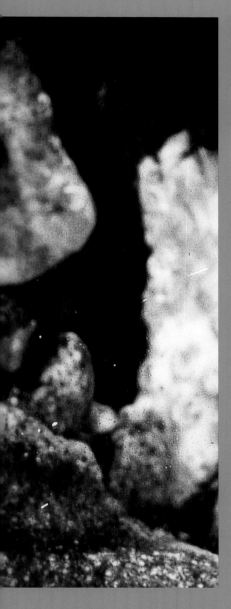

Chapter **7**

While books about freshwater aquaria often stress starting with a large aquarium, they are neither as adamant nor as liberal as marine books. While 20 gallons (75 liters) is often cited as a good size for a first freshwater tank, many authors insist on 40 gallons (150 liters) or even more for a first marine setup, with recommendations for reef aquaria being even larger. This gradation is not because marine tanks have different factors that influence success; it is because the margin for error in a marine system is even smaller than it is for freshwater setups. Several factors figure into this, including the nature of sea water relative to fresh water—for example, it holds less oxygen at a given temperature. Let's look at the major factors that argue for starting big and at how we need to approach them to apply the nano concept to saltwater aquaria.

Chemical Stability

At the core, maintaining an aquarium involves maintaining various chemical equilibria. When you put water into a tank, it has a certain chemistry, but because of the life processes that go on in it, that chemistry is always changing. Primary are temperature, pH, the concentration of various minerals, and the concentrations of waste products.

Aquarium fish differ greatly in their tolerance for a lack of equilibrium. Not surprisingly, their tolerance generally relates to the stability of their natural habitats. Species that migrate between different habitats and species from areas of great change, like estuaries or floodplains, adapt much better to aquarium life in general and to fluctuating water chemistry specifically. Fishes from relatively stable habitats are much more sensitive.

Since a larger volume of water changes temperature more slowly and can dilute waste products more than a small volume, a larger aquarium is more stable than a small one. If something goes wrong, the keeper of a large tank has more time to notice and remedy it before things become critical. This is the basis for all recommendations of starting big. But why are marine recommendations even higher?

Dissolved Nutrient Stability

The ocean—more specifically the tropical coral reef, from which habitat most marine ornamentals come—is one of the most stable habitats on Earth. Day in and day out, from season to season, there is little variation in temperature or water chemistry, and the fish that live there have little tolerance for fluctuation, or for conditions that are much less than pristine. The water teems with life of all kinds, but the water itself has extremely low concentrations of nutrients and wastes; everything is tied up in the biomass. As soon as an organism eliminates wastes, some other organism consumes those wastes.

The instant an aquarium is set up, however, nutrients and wastes begin to accumulate. Obviously, then, the larger the aquarium is, the more water there is into which wastes can dissolve—hence the benefit of starting big. In some very large reef systems full of live rock and invertebrates but with very few fish, there is an approximation of the natural reef ecosystem, and nutrient concentrations remain low. Even in these aquaria interventions such as protein skimming, chemical filtration, supplementation, and water changes are necessary to maintain pristine conditions, and to make up for calcium and alkalinity used up by animal growth. In systems with a higher bioload from fish, even more intervention is needed. A great deal of the paraphernalia associated with reef tanks—skimmers, kalkwasser, calcium reactors, ozonators, etc.—is involved with controlling water parameters within narrow ranges. In all cases, regular massive water changes would give similar or superior results, but that is rarely practical.

The size of a nano system, however, makes regular water change an appealing option. Large, frequent—even daily—water changes are usually not feasible on most marine setups, but they are eminently suited to nano tanks. A 50-percent weekly change on a 2-gallon (8-liter) tank will only require a 50-gallon bag of salt mix each year, an amount that would only provide a one-time 25-percent change on a moderately sized reef tank of 200 gallons (800 liters).

Such a large influx of freshly-made sea water on a regular basis will effectively dilute wastes, replace substances utilized by aquarium inhabitants (such as calcium taken up by growing corals), and keep mineral concentrations and pH at optimal levels. For many nano aquarists, this is the best option. You can even use the water removed from the tank to hatch brine shrimp to feed to your nano inhabitants.

pH Stability

Freshwater environments are found across a wide range of pH, from acidic black water and peat swamps to lakes with exceedingly high pH. The pH of ocean water, however, is boringly invariable at about 8.1. Not surprisingly, marine animals tend to be much less tolerant of fluctuations in pH than freshwater animals are.

The same metabolic processes that produce wastes also produce acids. This means that in any aquarium the pH will tend to drop over time. Sea water, whether natural or

synthetic, is highly buffered and can resist this pH drop for quite a while. In small volumes, however, the buffering capacity of the water is quickly exhausted, which is yet another reason for recommending a large aquarium for a marine setup. Fortunately, the feasibility of frequent water changes in a nano tank makes keeping up the buffering capacity of the water relatively simple. If the buffering capacity is not kept up, however, rapid and fatal pH drops are likely.

Ammonia/Ammonium Stability

Ammonia can dissolve in water as a gas: NH_3. It also undergoes ionization in water, becoming ammonium: NH_4^+. Usually when aquarists speak of "ammonia" they are not differentiating and are referring to both forms. The relative amounts of each depend on temperature and pH, and there is a significant difference in the toxicity of these two species, with gaseous ammonia being much more dangerous than ammonium.

Unfortunately for the marine hobbyist, the high pH and alkalinity of sea water mean that dissolved gaseous ammonia will be much more prevalent than ammonium ions. Thus, an equivalent biomass will produce more dangerous ammonia in a saltwater tank than in a freshwater one with neutral to acidic pH. Once again, this argues for a larger rather than smaller setup in order to provide more water into which ammonia wastes can be diluted, and it argues for an even larger setup for marine than for fresh.

For the nano aquarist, this translates into the increased importance of light stocking, optimum biofiltration, and regular large water changes.

Physical Stability

Several physical factors are important to consider. The first of these is a most crucial concern when maintaining a very small aquarium and was covered in Chapter 2: thermal stability. Though there is not much difference between the thermal stability of fresh versus salt water, the very narrow temperature range most marine ornamentals experience in their natural habitat makes temperature regulation even more important for the marine nano tank. Most freshwater species experience fluctuations from day to night, from season to season, even from one location to another as they move through their habitat; saltwater fish rarely encounter temperature differences.

The physics of aquaria come into play in two other significant ways when comparing fresh and marine: salt water can hold less dissolved oxygen than fresh water, and only water evaporates.

Dissolved Oxygen Stability

Naturally occurring non-aquatic low oxygen environments are extremely rare. On the other hand, the dissolved oxygen (DO) level in aquatic habitats is extremely variable and extremely important to living organisms. Under the best of circumstances, water cannot hold much DO, and even the highest possible concentrations of DO (about 10 ppm) are about 20,000 times lower than the atmospheric value of about 21 percent oxygen.

Atmospheric vs. Dissolved Oxygen
Oxygen in air = 21%
21 parts per hundred (percent) =
210 parts per thousand (permil) =
2100 parts per ten thousand =
21,000 parts per hundred thousand =
210,000 parts per million (ppm).
Maximum aquatic DO = 10 ppm.
210,000 ppm divided by 10 ppm = 21,000 times as much oxygen.

The saturation of DO varies inversely with temperature and with salinity: the higher the temperature, the lower the DO, and the higher the salinity, the lower the DO. Thus, the water in a tropical marine tank holds the least oxygen of all aquarium types, while that in a cold freshwater system holds the most.

Salinity Stability

Despite the fact that a quadrillion gallons or more evaporate from the world's oceans every day, the salinity of sea water varies very little. Near the mouths of large rivers it is a bit lower, and far from land in hot climes where evaporation is greater it is a bit higher, but for the most part the amount of dissolved salt is constant at a specific gravity of about 1.023 to 1.025.

This contrasts harshly with the situation in an aquarium, where daily evaporation can be quite significant. Since only water evaporates, leaving all dissolved substances behind, as the water level decreases the salinity in the aquarium increases. Evaporation must be replaced with fresh, preferably reverse-osmosis or deionized, water.

Fish Stability

Several factors figure in the compatibility of a fish with its tank and with its tankmates. Aside from the absolute size and biomass of a fish, its habits and behaviors can put various strains on the system. This is true in a setup of any size, but behavior that is of minor concern in a large reef tank might be unmanageable in a desktop system. Let's look at the major fish-based concerns in terms of the nano setup.

Predation

Predation is always a problem in marine systems. Few people would put a damsel in with a moray eel, unless it was intentionally to feed the eel, but often predator-prey relationships are much less obvious, and not always unidirectional. That is, a species may prey upon another at a certain point in its life cycle but be preyed upon by that same species at another point. Often, who eats whom is simply a basis of size; any fish will eat another fish if it is small enough to ingest. On the other hand, some fish can eat much larger fish by tearing them to pieces first. Fish-on-fish predation, however, is not much of a problem in nano tanks, simply because any fish included have to be quite tiny and inoffensive.

The majority of surprise predation in marine tanks is on small invertebrates—the snails, crabs, and worms that aquarists keep as scavengers. Many fish will happily dine on these animals, and hobbyists can be fooled by the small size at which some fish can get themselves a seafood snack. More aggressive predators will tear an invertebrate into bite- sized chunks. Invertebrates themselves often prey on each other. The larger a tank is, the more hiding places it provides, and there is less proximity of a predator and a potential prey item over time. This means that incidental predation will be greater in a nano system.

If specimens of the same size are kept in a nano tank, there is little chance of fish-on-fish predation. Aggression, however, is another matter, and some fish must be kept in a single-specimen tank.

Gramma loreto. This fish is extremely aggressive towards conspecifics and is best kept one per tank.

Aggression

Sometimes it seems that coral reef fishes live to kill members of their own species. Even fish that are found in massive aggregations in the wild often will not tolerate a conspecific in an aquarium. Some go so far as to attack any fish that looks the least bit similar to itself, and a few are so territorial they simply attack any other fish in the tank. The larger the tank, the more likely such a territorial specimen will leave some of the tank footprint out of its territory, making it possible to keep other specimens with it.

A few species, like some damsels, can often be managed in groups, in which aggression is diffused among all the members, while two or three individuals might fight endlessly. Nevertheless, the idea of using high stocking rates and providing plenty of hiding places just doesn't work out with marine species anywhere near as well as it does with, say, freshwater cichlids. One aquarist who tried it in an 8-foot (250-cm) reef tank with plenty of live rock nooks and crannies and a half dozen royal grammas, *Gramma loreto,* was soon down to one fish.

141

Live Rock Life

One of the exciting things about live rock is that you never know what will pop up in or on it. Sometimes even months after placing the rock into your tank you will see for the first time a coral, sponge, worm, or crab that came with the rock. The livestock diversity of Florida-aquacultured live rock is especially great, since this rock is often delivered to your door within days of being harvested from the ocean floor. Macroalgae and invertebrates, both sessile and motile, abound on this rock. It is even conceivable that a very small fish might survive the trip wedged into a crevice full of water. This suggests a fascinating application of the nano concept: a live rock tank. (We'll discuss this idea in the next chapter.)

A Larger Nano Concept

Taking all of these stability concerns into account, you can understand that marine aquarists often consider 20- to 30-gallon (80- to 120-liter) setups as nano tanks. Very small marine tanks—even reef systems—are possible, but we will also cover fish (and invertebrates in the next chapter) that require aquaria larger than most desktop units.

FOWLR

In the jargon of the marine hobby, tanks are classified as fish-only (FO), fish-only with live rock (FOWLR), or reef. It is generally accepted that live rock improves an aquarium containing just fish in the same way it improves one housing sessile reef invertebrates. The added biofiltration, including anoxic denitrification, helps maintain water quality; the encrusted rock provides a natural beauty as a background for the fish; and the organisms that grow on and among the rock provide the aquarium inhabitants with supplemental food. In a nano system, these benefits are especially welcome in maintaining stability.

The aesthetics of live rock can also be greater in a nano setup. The small organisms associated with live rock are, after all, perfectly suited to up-close observation. With only a few rocks in the aquarium, you will be able to keep track of each individually. From day to day there will be changes in the life on and around the rocks, but in most cases you will have to look closely to see it.

Gobies

With 2,000 species, there are certainly a lot of gobies to choose from, and many gobies make fine nano inhabitants. They tend to be small, fairly sedate, and peaceful, though there are exceptions. Many gobies are benthic, sticking fairly close to the substrate, but, again, there are exceptions, as you would expect in a group as large and diverse as this.

Some gobies in the genus *Amblyeleotris* can grow a bit larger than most fishes recommended in this book, but they are still acceptable because of their sedentary nature. Here one sits side-by-side with its shrimp burrowmate.

Figure 7.1

Gobies

Amblyeleotris gymnocephala

Cryptocentrus cinctus

Gobiodon sp.

A. wheeleri

Nemateleotris decora

Cryptocentrus sp.

C. leptocephalus

N. magnifica

Stonogobiops sp. (left)
Stonogobiops xanthorhinica (right)

Firefish

The firefish or dart fish of the genus *Nemateleotris* are such an example. These beautiful fish hover in mid water, never far from their favorite hidey hole. Both *N. magnifica* and *N. decora* are always available. Although they can usually be kept in pairs or small groups, you must be ready to intervene if the close quarters of a nano tank erodes their usually peaceful behavior.

Clown Gobies

Clown gobies of the genus *Gobiodon* are colorful and amusing—and tiny, with most species in the range of 35 to 65 mm (about an inch and a third to about two and a half inches). They are peaceful, even among themselves. Chubby, almost tadpole shaped, these peaceful fish have poisonous slime, so other fish usually leave them alone. However, they are not able to compete with aggressive feeders. In the wild they set up house among acroporid corals, on which they nibble and upon whose branches they string their eggs.

Neon Gobies

Perfect candidates for a nano system are the neon gobies of the genus *Elacatinus* (see Figure 7.2). The common neon, *E. oceanops,* has a thin, tapered body that can reach 50 mm (2 inches) with a bright blue neon stripe. It is one of the largest in the genus, and almost all species are perfect for a nano display. They generally get along well with each other, at least as mated pairs, and they are peaceful community members. Most if not all *Elacatinus* will serve as cleaners to their tankmates, but they can thrive without such a diet.

Figure 7.2
Neon Gobies

Elacatinus oceanops

E. puncticulatus

E. randalli

Mini-Aquariums

E. randalli is sometimes called the gold neon goby and looks like an *E. oceanops* with gold replacing the blue. Another fish also called the gold neon goby is *E. evelynae*. Hybrids between *randalli* and *oceanops* are being produced commercially, as well as hybrids of other species in this genus.

E. prochilos is a bit plumper and has a broader blue stripe, but otherwise it is very similar to *E. oceanops*. Both species have been successfully captive bred. Not really a neon goby, the red head goby *E. puncticulatus* is a popular aquarium species and perfect for a nano tank at about 44 mm (an inch an three quarters).

Shrimp Gobies

Shrimp or watchman gobies often form a commensal partnership with alpheid shrimp. The pair occupies a single burrow, which the virtually blind shrimp excavates and maintains. It keeps one antenna on its friend's back at all times so it can perceive the slightest twitch, and when the goby notices a potential predator, both shrimp and goby dash into the safety of the burrow. Most of the watchman gobies in the genera *Amblyeleotris* and *Cryptocentrus* range from 80 to 150 mm (about 3 to 6 inches), but their narrow bodies and sedentary behavior present less of a bioload than most fish that long. The shrimp gobies in the genus *Stonogobiops* are for the most part smaller and even more brightly colored with distinctive barring. Especially of note for a nano aquarium are *S. xanthorhinica* at 60 mm (two and a quarter inches) and *S. yasha* at 47 mm (under two inches).

Ctenogobiops tangaroai is a small (60 mm) goby that has been making its way into the hobby. Called by names such as masted shrimp goby and Tangaroa prawn-goby, this little shrimp goby is attractively spotted in red and white.

Basses

While many basses, family Serranidae, get too big for any aquarium—like the 9-foot (270-cm) giant grouper *Epinephelus*

Cryptocentrus sp.

lanceolatus—there are many species in this diverse group that are well suited to aquarium life, and of those several can be considered for larger nano systems, specifically those in the 10- to 20-gallon (40- to 80-liter) range. These small fish are sometimes called basslets or fairy basslets, but common names in this group seem especially capricious, and some species called "bass" are smaller than others routinely called "basslets" (see Figure 7.3).

One difficulty in assessing the suitability of these animals is that conflicting maximum sizes are often reported; the difference is sometimes considerable, say 3 versus 8 inches (75 versus 200 cm)! This is a result of varied experiences and occasional misidentifications, and it is important to keep alternative reports in mind when choosing

147

Liopropoma sp.

your specimens. If everyone agrees a fish stays under 3 inches (75 mm), it's a much safer bet than if some report larger maximum sizes.

All basslets are considered reef safe in that they will not normally prey on sessile invertebrates, but almost all will definitely eat small shrimp and worms. In fact, they are used by many aquarists to control bristleworm populations.

Liopropoma

The genus *Liopropoma* contains several desirable species, though their reclusive nature and deepwater habitats make them very expensive when they are available. These are torpedo-shaped fish, many with extensive horizontal striping. Perhaps the best known is the strikingly beautiful peppermint or Swiss Guard basslet, *L. rubre.* Even more dazzling is *L. carmabi*, often called the candy basslet. Both of these are in the 60- to 75-mm range (2 to 3inches). They are peaceful and retiring, but they will not tolerate conspecifics. The meteor perch or striped basslet, *L. susumi,* is a bit larger but otherwise similar. All of these fish are particularly suited for nano systems, as in a more typical reef tank they may thrive, but they will almost never be seen. The similar species *Lipogramma trilineatum* is another prime candidate but rarely available.

Do Your Homework

Many popular marine fish are, in fact, too large for home aquaria. Frequently a gorgeous juvenile grows into a drab, oversized adult. Since adult size and appearance are rarely given by ornamental fish retailers, these species continue to be sold in great numbers. The fish are often then doomed to stunting and/or early death. Some species either retain their juvenile colors or assume equally stunning appearance as adults but still grow too large for most systems. The prevalence in the market of fish that need at least a 200-gallon (800-liter) aquarium when grown is painfully greater than the prevalence of such large aquaria in the hobby. This means that the aquarist wishing to create a nano display has to be doubly careful to research a species before purchasing it.

Serranus

The genus *Serranus* has a few diminutive species that are available in the trade and suitable for a nano setup, including the chalk bass, *S. tortugarum*. This is one of the few popular marine species that can be maintained in groups, though that requires a large aquarium of 100 gallons (400 liters) or more. A single specimen could be the star of a nano display. This species is not so shy, and it tends to hover over its favorite hideaway, while many of its cousins prefer to hide most of the time.

Serranus baldwini, good only for larger marine nano setups.

Non-Bass Basslets

Probably the best known "basslet" is the royal gramma, *Gramma loreto*, which is in the family Grammatidae, not Serranidae. Small and impossibly colored—violet up front and yellow aft—it is a beautiful and relatively peaceable aquarium fish, provided the aquarium does not contain any other fish of similar

Figure 7.3

Basslets

Pseudochromis porphyreus

L. rubre

P. paccagnellae

Gramma melacara

L. susumi

Assessor flavissimus

Liopropoma carmabi

P. fridmani

Serranus tortugarum

The popular royal gramma, *Gramma loreto*.

shape or coloration, as royal grammas viciously defend their territories. Its deepwater relative, the black cap basslet or gramma, *Gramma melacara,* is just as striking with a deep purple body, black "cap," and white tail. At 4 inches (10 cm) it is a bit larger than the 3-inch (8-cm) royal gramma.

Other fish called "basslet" but not in the family Serranidae that can be featured in a desktop aquarium include the banded longfin basslet, *Belonepterygion fasciolatum.* On the other hand, the basslets known as anthias, genera *Anthias, Pseudanthias, Mirolabrichthys,* and others, cannot be kept in nano aquaria; they are difficult enough to maintain in large setups. Two other groups called basslets do have members that can be considered for a nano system: dottybacks (family Pseudochromidae) and assessors (family Plesiopidae).

Dottybacks

The common dottybacks of the genus *Pseudochromis* are extremely popular, and many species are available tank bred. *P. fridmani*, the orchid dottyback, is one of the more peaceful species (though still quite nasty), while the very similar looking purple dottyback, *P. porphyreus*, is an absolute terror, as is the royal-gramma-looking *P. paccagnellae*. Because of the vicious intolerance of these gorgeous species for just about any other fish, many people despair of ever enjoying them. Small, beautiful, and sociopathic? Sounds like a perfect combination for a one-fish nano system!

Assessors

Although not dottybacks, assessors are sometimes confused with them. Currently two species are being captive raised, *Assessor flavissimus*, the yellow assessor, which reaches 55 mm (2 inches) and *A. macneilli*, known as the blue assessor or blue devilfish, at 60 mm (2¼ inches). Though quite similar to dottybacks, assessors are generally peaceful fish, even with their own kind. It is wisest, however, to restrict them one to a tank when stocking nano setups.

Pseudochromis paccagnellae

Chrysiptera parasema

Damsels and Kin

Three groups of fish in the family Pomacentridae have species worthy of consideration for a nano display: damselfish, chromis, and clownfish.

Damsels

Damselfish are relatively small, reef-safe, colorful, hardy, and inexpensive. Damsels in the larger sense include clownfish and chromis, but we are speaking in the narrow sense here—all pomacentrids that are neither chromis nor clowns. A few species grow rather large and become drab as they mature, but most do not. Thus they are quite common in the hobby. The problem is that they are, as a group, hellions. Aggressive and territorial to the extreme, they can make life miserable for any other fish in the system, even much larger ones. As in any diverse group of fish, there are exceptions to the rules, and even the most aggressive specimens can make a successful one-fish nano display. In fact, you could populate a series of nano tanks each with one damsel in it and have a most colorful and interesting display.

There are many species of blue damsels that go under the common name of blue devils. As the name implies, these fish can be rather obnoxious, but their beauty can easily be taken advantage of in a nano tank in which they are the only fish. Some live rock and a few invertebrates can complete the display. There are also several species with deep blue bodies and yellow or orange tails. One of these, *Chrysiptera parasema*, is not very aggressive, and it can usually be kept in small groups in large tanks. In a nano, however, it is probably better to stick with one, though you should be able to include other types of fish with the one damsel.

Chromis

Several species in the genus *Chromis* are notable in that they can be kept in schools in the aquarium and are peaceful with each other and with other fish. The ever popular green chromis, *C. viridis,* and its blue congener *C. cyanea* are happy in groups and are rightfully considered schooling damsels. It is interesting, however, that some aquarists have reported problems with aggression between chromis in truly small tanks. Perhaps these fish simply have a much closer threshold than most marines—a large aggregation of dottybacks or tangs will do fine in a 10,000-gallon (38,000-liter) system but may fight to the death if more than one is kept in a normal home aquarium, and maybe chromis start to feel crowded more around the 5- to 10-gallon (20- to 40-liter) range. Their decreased territoriality (compared to most in the damsel group) makes it possible in most cases to keep one with other types of fish in a nano aquarium.

Chromis viridis (left)
C. cyanea (right)

Clownfish

Clowns are a special group within the damselfish family Pomacentridae; they are also known as anemonefish. In the wild these fish can survive only by living in a host anemone whose stinging tentacles protect them from predators. Many but not all of the anemone species that host clownfish must have resident clownfish in order to survive, as the fish drive off animals that want to eat the anemone. Unfortunately, as hardy and adaptable as clownfish are, the vast majority of anemones are completely unsuitable for the home aquarium. They are even less suitable for a nano system. On the other hand, clownfish in captivity do not need an anemone. Commercial clownfish breeders almost never provide anemones for their broodstock, and tank-raised clowns—the only kind you should consider buying—have never seen an anemone.

Clownfish are the darlings of the marine hobby, known to many people outside the hobby, even before one was featured in an animated movie. The best suited to a nano setup is a percula clown, either *Amphiprion percula* or *A. ocellaris*. Also to be considered is one of the many skunk clownfish, *A. perideraion*, which is often called the pink, salmon, or pink skunk clown and gets only a smidgeon larger than the perculas (see Figure 7.4). All three of these are small enough and peaceful enough for a nano setup, alone or with other peaceful fish. The other clownfish, although available as tank-raised specimens, are too large or aggressive for a nano system.

The clownfish are all protandrous hermaphrodites—every "family" contains a large female, a smaller male, and perhaps one or more immature fish. Until something happens to one of them, things remain static, but an immature fish can become a functional male, and a male will become the female if something happens to the group's female. A pair can be kept in a tank of 20 gallons (80 liters) or so.

Remember, although the clownfish-anemone symbiosis is fascinating, anemones are generally not recommended for home aquaria, as they have dismal survival records in most cases.

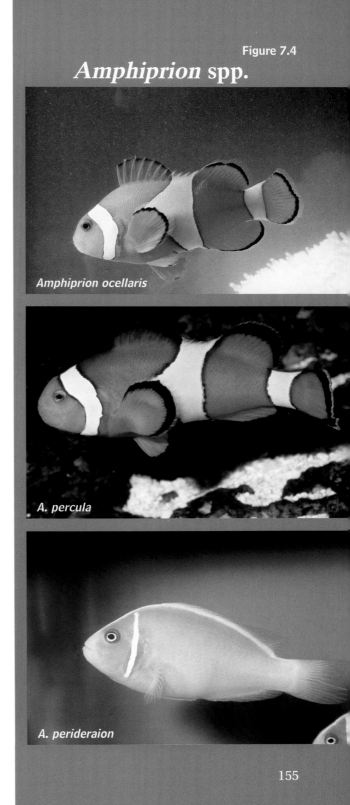

Figure 7.4

Amphiprion spp.

Amphiprion ocellaris

A. percula

A. perideraion

True or False?

One of the most persistent unfounded beliefs in the aquarium hobby is that common names can be right or wrong. Actually, there is absolutely no control over common names, and they can vary in their application from individual to individual, from group to group, from region to region, and from language to language.

The fish now known as *Amphiprion ocellaris* was originally brought into the hobby as *A. percula*. When that very similar species was brought into the hobby, the original clownfish became known as the "false percula clown." The new one was called the "true percula clown." Even though the common name is taken from the scientific name, as soon as it is applied as a common name it is no longer under any control. In the confusion both species have been called perculas, both with and without the "true" or "false" designations. There is nothing negative about *A. ocellaris*; it's simply a matter of a mistaken identification on our part, and neither species is more true or false than the other.

Husbandry techniques have improved, though, and some aquarists have anemones reproducing by division in their tanks (though division can also be a last-ditch effort by a dying animal). In any case, a nano setup is not the place for an anemone, but your clownfish will do fine without an invertebrate host.

Amphiprion ocellaris and its host anemone. In the wild, a clownfish does not stray far from its anemone.

Angelfish

The diverse and ever popular marine angels are ruled by the majestic fish in the genus *Pomacanthus*. Most of these beauties are too large for all but the hugest home aquaria, but the dwarf angels of the genus *Centropyge* scale down the grace and beauty of angelfish to a size where many species can be considered for tanks as small as 10 to 20 gallons (40 to 80 liters).

No *Centropyge* can be considered completely reef safe, though aquarists report vastly different experiences. In a nano system, however, it would be foolish to expect the fish not to nibble on corals, as they are grazers. If you want a desktop reef, it would be best to leave out the angel, but for a FOWLR setup you should consider this group strongly. While angels in this genus are often kept in small groups in large systems, in the close quarters of a desktop tank, only one *Centropyge* specimen should be housed. And that desktop tank should be mature, with natural algae growth, to keep the fish at its healthiest.

The smallest in the genus (3 inches or 8 cm), the pygmy angel, *C. argi*, is widely available and inexpensive. It can be kept in systems as small as 10 gallons (40 liters), but such a setup should include a single angel as the only fish, as this is an aggressive little fish.

Only about an inch (2 cm) larger, the coral beauty or two-spined angel, *C. bispinosa,* is usually tolerant of smaller fish. About the same size, the ever popular flame angel, *C. loricula,* is, if anything, even more peaceful, and its beauty and hardiness are appreciated by many aquarists (see Figure 7.5). In fact, this was one of the first dwarf angels to be bred in captivity.

Moray Eels

You probably did a double take when you saw this heading. A moray in a nano? Well, with hundreds of species (more than 100 in the genus *Gymnothorax* alone) it makes sense that at least one would be suitable for certain nano setups. That one is not easy to find, and it will probably cost you a couple of hundred dollars or

Figure 7.5

Dwarf Angels

Centropyge bispinosa

C. loricula

C. argi

157

more, but *Gymnothorax melatremus*, the appropriately named dwarf moray, tops out at 8 to 10 inches (20 to 25 cm). Because of its long, thin body type, that doesn't add up to very much fish flesh. Add its sedentary lifestyle, and you have a moray eel that can be housed satisfactorily in a 10-gallon (40-liter) or larger nano system. The predatory abilities of this eel are scaled down with its size, so fish and shrimp larger than its open gape are safe, but do not scale down your vigilance in preventing escape. This eel can slither out of the tiniest openings, and that would be one expensive hunk of rug jerky!

Hippocampus zosterae will wrap its tail around a perch and wait for food to come to it.

Syngnathids

Small tanks are often recommended for seahorses, genus *Hippocampus*. These fish are largely passive predators that wait anchored by their prehensile tail for the currents to bring tiny prey items to them. When they hunt actively, they hover around, painstakingly picking off small invertebrates that they find. Until captive-bred specimens were widely available most seahorses would only accept living food items, so restricting aquarium size kept the prey in close proximity to the slow-moving fish. Today a wide variety of species are available as captive-bred fish trained to accept frozen *Mysis* shrimp.

The seahorse most suited for a small desktop setup is the dwarf *H. zosterae*, which grows at most to 50 mm (under 2 inches). This US native is quite hardy, and a small herd can be maintained in a 5-gallon (20-liter) nano system. This fish is an exception when it comes to keeping it with live rock or live sand. Hydroids that commonly arrive with these substrates can wipe out your dwarf ponies very quickly. They are simply too small to deal with the venom of these invertebrates. The fish are found in the wild in seagrass beds, where they feed on tiny shrimp. Macroalgae or plastic plants can provide both security and hitching locations for the seahorses, which will grasp them with their prehensile tails.

Dwarf seahorses can subsist on a diet of enriched baby brine shrimp, which is suitable both for adults and for their relatively large newborn fry. As with other seahorses, it is the male dwarf that gets pregnant and gives birth to the babies, and it is common for aquarists to raise generation after generation of these fascinating fish.

Pipefish, which are very much like horizontal seahorses, can also be considered for larger nano displays. Like their vertical cousins, they cannot compete with aggressive feeders, but they can make good tankmates for seahorses.

Blennies

The name "blenny" is applied rather loosely to fish of a number of families that share certain characteristics such as benthic habit, reduced or absent swim bladder, and large eyes and mouths. The group also includes the wolf eel *Anarrhichthys ocellatus,* which grows to 250 cm (8½ feet)! Sometimes certain gobies and dragonets are also called blennies. With fish in this group ranging from tiny to behemoth, and with common names being whimsically applied in many cases, it is especially important to research any fish you are considering buying. Many blennies are perfect for a nano, but many others will outgrow the tank almost overnight!

Ecsenius and *Meiacanthus*

These two genera of combtooth blennies contain some great little species. The bicolor blenny *E. bicolor* at 110 mm (just over 4 inches) is fairly peaceful and can be kept with damsels, dwarf angels, dottybacks, etc., but not with meek species like many of the gobies. The similar mimic blenny *E. gravieri* at 80 mm (just over 3 inches) is another fish that will spend most of its time among the live rock, but individuals appreciate open swimming room as well.

Ecsenius bicolor

Ecsenius midas

Both are largely herbivorous and need algae to be the base of their diet.

E. bandanus (34 mm) and *E. trilineatus* (30 mm) are often seen. They and other small blennies are all potential candidates.

The Midas blenny *E. midas* is appropriately golden colored and attains about 130 mm (5 inches). It spends most of its time up in the water and is a planktonivore that often schools with other species. It can be aggressive, so it might be best to use it in a single-specimen nano system.

The (poison) fang blennies of the genus *Meiacanthus* are named for the pair of venomous fangs that give most predators pause. These fish must be handled with extreme care. Like many other venomous animals, these fish are usually peaceful, willing to live and let live, secure in the knowledge they can protect themselves if needed. Research the sizes for species you find available, as some are too big for nano setups, but many are fine for larger nanos.

Imitation as a Means of Survival

It is very common to find pairs of species, one a fang blenny and another that mimics the venomous member of the pair. An example is the venomous *Meiacanthus grammistes* (left) and the harmless mimic *Petroscirtes breviceps* (right). The non-venomous species is protected by the other's reputation.

Cardinals

Cardinalfish are named for the deep red color several species display, though some of the most popular species are not red at all. These are fish of the dark that prefer to spend the brightest hours in a cave or under an overhang, coming out during dusk and dark. For the most part they are communal, appreciating and gathering with other members of their species, and they are paternal mouthbrooders. The male holds the eggs in his mouth until the young are able to swim. Unlike most other marine fish, some cardinals do not have a planktonic larval stage but emerge from their father's throat as fully developed miniatures of the adults.

Three genera figure in the aquarium trade. *Apogon* has over 200 species, many of which are available at least occasionally (see Figures 7.6 and 7.7). Some that are particularly well suited to a nano system are:
- *A. coccineus* 60 mm (about 2$\frac{1}{2}$ inches)
- *A. cyanosoma* 80 mm (just over 3 inches)
- *A. dispar* 50 mm (2 inches)
- *A. maculatus* 111 mm (about 4$\frac{1}{3}$ inches)
- *A. multilineatus* 100 mm (4 inches)
- *A. nigripes* 70 mm (2$\frac{3}{4}$ inches)
- *A. nigripinnis* 100 mm (4 inches)
- *A. novemfasciatus* 100 mm (4 inches)
- *A. opercularis* 70 mm (2$\frac{3}{4}$ inches)

Pterapogon kauderni is one of two species in the genus (the other, *P. mirifica*, is not seen in the aquarium trade). Known as the Banggai cardinal, this fish became very popular some years back and soon was reported overfished and becoming endangered. Since it so easily bred in the aquarium, there is no longer any reason to purchase wild-caught specimens.

Sphaeramia, the third genus, has two similar species: *Sphaeramia nematoptera* at 85 mm (under 3$\frac{1}{2}$ inches) and *S. orbicularis* at 100 mm (4 inches). At this size they are best for larger nanos, but they are commonly available, inexpensive, and peaceful (see Figure 7.7).

Figure 7.6

Apogon spp.

Apogon sp.

A. cyanosoma

A. maculatus

A. multilienatus

Figure 7.7

Cardinalfish

Cardinals offer many opportunities for stocking a larger marine nano. These mouthbrooding fish come in a variety of shapes and colors.

Apogon nigripes

A. novemfasciatus

Pterapogon kauderni

Sphaeramia nematoptera

S. orbicularis

163

Wrasses

The family Labridae is one of the largest fish families, with more than 600 species in over 60 genera. This diverse group ranges from the tiny (60-mm, 2-inch) *Minilabrus striatus* to the gargantuan Napoleon wrasse *Cheilinus undulatus* at 2290 mm (7$\frac{1}{2}$ feet) and 191.0 kg (420 pounds)! There are peaceful, reef-safe wrasses and nasty, predatory wrasses. It would be generous to call some wrasses drab, while others are riotously colored. Not surprisingly with such variability, there are wrasses for just about any aquarium setup, including a nano tank. Let's look at some desktop wrasses alphabetically genus by genus (see Figure 7.8).

Bodianus

Known as hogfish, the wrasses in this genus are a bit large for nano systems, but the popular twospot hogfish, *B. bimaculatus,* reaches only 100 mm (just under 4 inches) and is suitable for the largest nanos, especially as a single specimen.

Cirrhilabrus

Several of the fairy or velvet wrasses of this planktonivorous genus are small enough to consider for larger nano systems. They are extremely colorful and display sexual dichromatism. Although many can be kept in groups, especially haremic groups, in large aquaria, you should restrict yourself to only one wrasse of any kind in a nano aquarium. *C. aurantidorsalis* reaches 90 mm (3$\frac{1}{2}$ inches). The recently (2002) described *C. bathyphilus* maxes out at 76 mm (just under 3 inches), and *C. condei* at 80 mm (just over 3 inches), the same as *C. filamentosus*. *C. flavidorsalis* is extremely colorful, even for a fairy wrasse, and it grows to only 65 mm (2$\frac{1}{2}$ inches). *C. johnsoni* is even smaller, at 60 mm (2$\frac{1}{3}$ inches). *C. marjorie* is 58 mm (2$\frac{1}{4}$ inches), and *C. pylei* is 90 mm (3$\frac{1}{2}$ inches). *C. rubripinnis* reaches 91 mm (3$\frac{1}{2}$ inches), while *C. rubrisquamis* is a bit smaller at 72 mm (2$\frac{3}{4}$ inches), and *C. rubriventralis* is 75 mm (2$\frac{3}{4}$ inches).

Doratonotus

This monotypic (only one species in it) genus is represented by *D. megalepis,* known as the dwarf wrasse even though at 94 mm (less than 3$\frac{3}{4}$ inches) it is not the smallest wrasse by any means. Since it is a Caribbean species, it would be easy to bring in for the US trade, but its lack of bright colors makes it often overlooked.

Figure 7.8

Wrasses

Bodianus bimaculatus

C. rubrisquamis

Pseudocheilinus hexataenia

Cirrhilabrus aurantidorsalis

C. rubriventralis

P. tetrataenia

C. rubripinnis

Halichoeres chrysus

Figure 7.9

Paracheilinus spp.

Male flasher wrasses balance attracting mates and avoiding predators by confining their nuptial displays to a few seconds, after which they zip back into the rocks for safety.

Paracheilinus filamentosus

P. lineopunctatus

Halichoeres

This is a large and diverse genus of mostly large wrasses. A couple species could be suitable for nano systems, like *H. binotopsis* at 89 mm (3½ inches). *H. chrysus*, often called by the misleading name of "yellow coris wrasse" (it is not in the genus *Coris*) is a peaceful, reef-safe species of about 100 mm (4 inches).

Paracheilinus

The flasher wrasses of this genus (see Figure 7.9) get their common name from both their flashy colors and the flashing behavior of the males—they zoom up from their hiding places, flash their flamboyant colors and fins, then dive back into their hideaways. Almost all species are 3 inches or less (under 80 mm), and they are peaceful planktonivores. A large number of species are available, though not always identified. These are reef safe with almost any invertebrates and peaceful with other fish. A single male and a couple of females will coexist, but the aquarium would have to be at least 20 gallons (80 liters).

Pseudocheilinus

Even mild aggression can be disastrous in the extreme enclosure of a nano aquarium. The lined wrasses in this genus are small and beautiful, but they are potential aggressors, and they will definitely prey on small motile invertebrates. A few common species get a bit large, but as they are aggressive you might want only to keep a single specimen, so it can be a little larger and still work in a nano.

Wetmorella

Wetmorella nigropinnata

The arrowhead or sharpnose wrasses, two species in this genus, are often available and are very good candidates for a nano setup. These fish come from fairly deep waters and live in caves. This means that in a normal reef system they will rarely be seen, but in a nano they can be stars. A live-rock cave whose opening faces front will enable the fish to hide in plain sight. *W. albofasciata* gets about 60 mm (less than 2½ inches) long, and *W. nigropinnata* about 80 mm (just over 3 inches).

Figure 7.10

Hawkfish

Hawkfish do not need a lot of swimming room. Like their namesakes, they perch up on the reef, keenly scanning for something edible. When they spot their prey, they dive headlong for it.

Neocirrhites armatus

Oxycirrhites typus

Cirrhitichthys falco

Hawkfish

The smaller hawkfish are great for nanos. Due to their sedentary lifestyle, they can be included at larger sizes than more active fish. A great display would be a hawkfish with a live-rock perch in the center of the tank. One or two bottom-dwelling and midwater fish would complete the setup. The hawkfish would survey its realm from its high vantage, always ready to pounce upon possible tidbits. Hawkfish are generally peaceful towards anything they cannot swallow, but they do tend to dominate, so tankmates should be feisty enough not to be bullied. They do not tolerate conspecifics, and they will prey on any bite-sized fish or invertebrates.

Cirrhitichthys falco, the falco or dwarf hawkfish, reaches only 70 mm (2³/4 inches) and is commonly available. It is probably the best behaved of the group. *Neocirrhites armatus*, the popular flame hawkfish, tops out at 90 mm (3¹/2 inches) and can be nasty. In the confines of a nano it would be best as a single fish. For setups on the larger end of the nano spectrum, the longnose hawkfish, *Oxycirrhites typus*, at 130 mm (just over 5 inches), can be considered—again best as a single fish (see Figure 7.10).

Perchlets

The perchlets in the genus *Plectranthias* are not hawkfish, though they are sometimes sold as such. They are relatives of the anthias, which cannot be considered for a nano system, but the perchlets can be included in many nano setups. Showing remarkable similarities in form and behavior with actual hawkfish, many of the numerous species in this genus are 45 mm (1³/4 inches) or less, and none of them is very large. Most are colorful candidates for a desktop tank.

Jawfish

One of the most commonly available species in the genus *Opistognathus*, the yellowhead or pearly jawfish, *O. aurifrons,* is a possible nano candidate. These fish need a deep sandbed—at least 5 cm (2 inches)—to burrow into. Although they can usually be kept in small groups in a large tank, in a nano they should be kept singly. Depending on the size of the tank, a peaceful non-jawfish tankmate or two is possible.

Watching an *Opistognathus aurifrons* create its burrow is a fascinating process. It takes portions of the substrate into its mouth, and then spits it out away from its new home, until a sufficiently deep hole has been dug.

169

Specimen Display

Sometimes what appears to be a good candidate for a specimen display is not. Consider the mandarin or dragonet *Synchiropus*. The fish is small (60 to 70 mm, 2 to 2¾ inches) and while not actually sedentary, it is benthic, and it hops around the reef, not requiring any real swimming room. These fish, however, are poor candidates for any aquarium because of the difficulty in providing them with appropriate types and quantities of food. The few that thrive in captivity are in huge mature reef systems where a stable population of amphipods and other small prey items provides the proper diet. Therefore the smallest aquarium that can adequately house a single mandarin is probably about 200 gallons (800 liters) in most cases.

On the other hand, consider the frogfish *Antennarius maculatus*. This is a heavy-bodied predator that can consume fish almost its own size! Although one of the smallest species of its type, it grows to about 100 mm (4 inches), so it seems to be out of the question for a nano setup. Nevertheless, since this fish is likely to consume any other fish kept with it, even a conspecific, and since it is an ambush predator that rarely swims and merely creeps around the bottom on pectoral-fin "feet," it is a potential candidate for an unusual and interesting nano specimen display of at least 10 gallons (40 liters). Any tank that small will require frequent large water changes in addition to

Despite its small size, *Synchiropus picturatus* is a difficult specimen to keep and should only be placed in very large tanks with established live rock for it to feed on.

good filtration and skimming, but it is an ideal way to display this unusual animal. In addition, the fish is cryptically colored, looking much like a lump of live rock. Such camouflage serves the fish very well in the wild, but in a large aquarium with plenty of live rock, it will tend to disappear. As a nano specimen, however, it will be one of only a couple of pieces of rock, so the nano focus will spotlight its invisibility!

Community Display

Since marine fish must be kept at lower stocking densities than freshwater fish, it figures that a marine nano is not going to be much of a community. This is true even considering that saltwater nano systems are larger than most freshwater nanos, especially when you factor in the high aggression levels of many popular marine species. In fact, we have repeatedly recommended fish for single-specimen setups in this chapter.

Still, a community is possible. A 10-gallon (40-liter) aquarium could house a pair of neon gobies, perhaps a small damsel, and some peppermint shrimp. A 30-gallon (115-liter) tank could be stocked with a pair of percula clowns, a royal gramma, and maybe three small cardinals. So it can be done; just make sure to consider adult size and temperament when selecting fish to include.

Biotope Display

One biotope ideally suited for a nano display is the tidepool. Tidepool organisms are among the hardiest, since they have to endure extremes in temperature, dissolved oxygen, and salinity in their habitat. Tropical tidepool fish and invertebrates are not common in the hobby, but if you have access to a temperate tidepool and can legally collect organisms from it, you could have a fascinating display.

Generally, however, the biotope concept with marine or reef tanks is simply to combine fish and invertebrates that can be found on the same reefs in the wild. This proscribes, for example, mixing clownfish (Indo-Pacific) and royal grammas (Caribbean). A nano system makes it possible to focus on a much smaller biotope, a microhabitat. Just one example would be to have an acroporid coral colony and a couple of clown gobies *Gobiodon* sp.

Tops Stop!

Any fish can jump out of an aquarium, but certain species are much more likely to. In fact, some can almost be said to be guaranteed to jump out. Many of the fish discussed in this chapter are in this category. When you factor in the tighter quarters of a nano system, that guarantee is just about ironclad. Make sure that your tank is completely covered and that any necessary holes or access ports are sealed with nylon mesh or some other barrier.

171

Marine Invertebrates

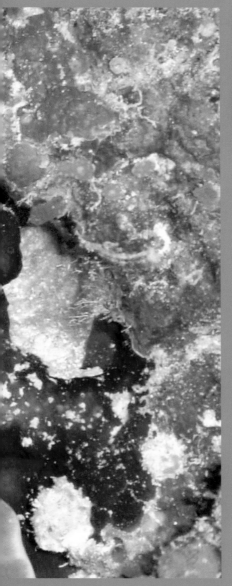

Chapter **8**

In large part, it is the nano reef aquarium that has fueled the rise in popularity of the desktop tank. The nano reef itself has a basis in a component of the nano concept that plays a negligible part in most other types of systems: control. The precision with which water parameters can be controlled in modern marine setups makes the nano reef a badge of honor. While even large marine systems were until recently quite difficult to stabilize, the knowledge and technology have progressed to the point that there are successful one-gallon (4-liter) reefs! All the other considerations—beauty, ornament, and natural microcosm—are certainly part of the nano reef, but it also is a testament to the skills of the aquarist. Although harder to maintain than larger systems, the nano reef has a big advantage: it makes the reef aquarium affordable to many more people. Ironically, however, nano reefs of this kind are not the focus of this book. Rather, the application of the nano concept to other types of aquaria is what we are promoting, especially reefs that have a focus on invertebrates other than on corals and anemones. The reason for this is simply that it is much better to move down from a regular reef tank to a nano reef. We will provide the basics of establishing and maintaining a typical nano reef, but we strongly encourage you to get experience with reef systems prior to trying one. In the meantime, we provide several ideas for less traditional nano reefs as well.

The Nano Reef

Even though there was never a firm distinction between "nano reefs" and "pico reefs," and even though the use of the term "pico" seems to be fading, the original mini-/micro-nano-pico gradation has left its mark: many reef aquarists speak of reef tanks up to at least 30 gallons (120 liters) as nano reefs. This is especially true if an all-in-one unit is used. These cubic—or at least square—aquaria offer maximum area for arranging live rock and invertebrates, as well as maximum use of the high-intensity lighting fixtures.

An Inexpensive Reef

It is not uncommon for reef aquarists to spend five-figure sums on a single aquarium. The live rock alone can cost more than $1,000, as can a lighting system. The hobbyist can be in the hole for several thousand dollars before adding the first animal! Then maintenance requires either specialized equipment or lots of water changes, both of which cost a lot of money. The cost of skimmers, calcium reactors, dosing pumps, controllers, etc., must be weighed against the cost of buckets upon buckets of salt mix.

Now compare that to a desktop reef setup. When only a few pounds of live rock are needed, you can splurge on the quality. Lights with even 10 watts per gallon are not extravagant when you're dealing with a system of only a couple of gallons. Since large water changes are very feasible on nano marine tanks, it is possible to maintain the proper water parameters without using complex equipment, additives, and constant testing. Even protein skimming, which almost all reef aquarists insist on, becomes optional with sufficient water changes. The point is that you cannot skimp in your dedication. A nano reef of only a few gallons with SPS (small-polyp stony) corals is certainly possible, and one good way to pull it off is to change half the water every day. That simple chore can eliminate the need for skimming, water testing, calcium supplementation, etc., but without those aids there is no margin for laxness—missing a single water change might spell disaster. The only cost outlay, however, is salt mix in relatively small quantities.

12-gallon (48-liter) nano reef. Several *Actinodiscus* sp. mushrooms in red, purple/blue, and green. Large *Aiptasia* anemone. Encrusting yellow sponge (unknown genus) on rock. Large colony of grape *Caulerpa*. *Palythoa*, brown button polyps. One fish, *Amblyglyphidodon leucogaster*. Mixed cleanup crew consisting of four blue- and red-legged hermit crabs, one margarita snail.

Even the livestock comes cheaply for the nano reef. A $65 fish you're afraid will be eaten up in a large tank—or at least disappear into the live rock only to be viewed on rare occasion—can be the prized sole inhabitant of a nano. Two or three small coral frags can make a beautiful display in a desktop reef, comparable to a single specimen costing tens of times as much in a standard size reef.

A Focused Reef

The double focus of a nano reef (the reef tank focuses on the coral reef, the nano reef focuses on that focus) allows an aquarist to take a microscope to the dynamics of a reef. I once sat enthralled in front of a reef aquarium, watching a tiny blue-legged hermit crab painstakingly climb a rock formation, jump off, and float to the bottom, only to repeat the behavior over and over. Its purpose never became evident, but its dedication and zeal were, and I wouldn't be surprised to learn that it was doing this just for the fun of it—it certainly seemed to be enjoying itself! Watching the feeding behavior of coral polyps can be equally fascinating, and although there are occasional blink-and-you'll-miss-it moments, much of it appears in slow motion, which adds to the otherworldly feeling.

With a desktop reef you will witness many more such events, first because the small tank necessarily focuses your attention, but also because you can steal glances repeatedly during the day, greatly increasing your chances of catching behaviors that don't occur that often. A desktop reef also provides an opportunity that is rarely taken with larger setups, to concentrate on the incredible diversity of life that is found in natural reefs on the micro level. In a real sense, such a nano tank is an outgrowth of sump technology.

Elevating the Sump

At first reef aquarists used sumps to increase the volume of their system. A 90-gallon (340-liter) tank might be plumbed into a 200-gallon (760-liter) vat in the basement. The filtration, skimming, and heating equipment are installed on the vat, keeping it out of sight. The total volume is 290 gallons (1,100 liters), so many more animals can be kept in the aquarium than would otherwise be possible, and the water quality is much easier to maintain.

Aquarists have a hard time leaving empty vats of water, however, so the refugium was born—a second volume, plumbed into the display tank, but lighted and outfitted with live rock and sand, and often macroalgae or even mangroves. The refugium not only provides greater volume for increased capacity and water stability but also adds to filtration (live rock, live sand, harvesting macroalgae) and provides a predator-free haven where plankton (small inverts and the gametes and larvae of larger inverts) can proliferate (which are then pumped back to the display tank to feed the animals there). When its lighting cycle is the reverse of the lighting on the main tank, this helps to stabilize pH and DO levels, since photosynthesis is continuous in one of the pair or the other.

Well, it's also hard for most aquarists to have a lighted volume of water with just live rock and tiny critters, and many use the refugium as a temporary home for juvenile or injured fish, or to safely house interesting animals that would decimate the reef invertebrates in the main display, or to safely house interesting animals that would be killed by the animals in the main display.

The next logical step, of course, is to maintain a refugium-style tank independent of another display. This isn't very commonly done, mainly because the idea of maintaining a large aquarium with just some live-sand inverts and copepods among the live rock isn't too exciting. Why? Because those animals are so small. You've got to look closely, maybe even with a magnifying glass, to see them. Hence, they're perfect for a nano setup!

Live Rock Nano

A desktop tank set up with just live rock should, over time, become teeming with marine life. It will change from day to day, with some plants and animals dying off and other ones taking hold. Without fish or "cleanup crew" invertebrates to prey on them, the live rock organisms will flourish and provide a display visible only on the nano level—you will have to look closely to see what's going on, and you'll be able to track the growth of individual specimens from their almost microscopic beginnings. Many reef hobbyists keep a magnifying glass handy; with a desktop nano you will want one permanently next to the tank.

Nighttime brings a whole other world to the reef, and to a reef tank. Invertebrates that spend the day soaking up sunshine for their photosynthetic symbionts play out feeding tentacles to trap plankton. Creatures that hide out of sight all day emerge for night prowls, while many daytime denizens of the reef disappear into the nooks and crannies or even under the sand to sleep. The water itself often glows as a multitude of luminescent organisms—many microscopic—produce light in a natural marvel we terrestrials usually see only in the limited scope of fireflies and an occasional fungus.

One of the treats of keeping live rock is not really knowing what may be living in all of its nooks and grooves. Given time, you just may find out.

Motile Inverts

All of the inverts, save insects, that make good freshwater aquarium inhabitants are represented in much greater number by marine relatives. In addition, there are many marine invertebrates without freshwater counterparts—cephalopods, nudibranchs, and echinoderms, for example. The vastly greater numbers of species means there are many more to choose from, and the chances are very good that you can find just the right invertebrates for the nano system you wish to create.

As with freshwater inverts, the nano tank permits you to focus on small animals that are easily lost in the vast bustle of a regular marine aquarium. The tiny snails and hermit crabs that are widely used as cleanup crews for reef tanks are colorful and fascinating, but 50 hermits in a 100-gallon (400-liter) tank full of live rock and corals are not likely to be a focal point. On the other hand, a half dozen in a 5-gallon (20-liter) desktop with a pile of live rock rubble could provide a lot of enjoyment with their antics.

Because of the diversity in each of these groups, it is vital that you research any species before purchasing it. There are small, peaceful, reef-safe crabs, shrimps, and snails, but there are also large, aggressive, predatory, and coralivorous species of each. Size itself is not the only criterion—there are carnivorous snails that will prey on larger snails, as well as cannibalistic hermit crabs that will ignore algae and detritus in favor of their comrades. Some omnivorous species will seek the easiest meal; once all the algae is gone, they may turn on their tankmates.

Crustaceans

There are a great number of species of crabs, shrimp, and lobsters available for marine tanks, as well as various amphipods and copepods that are usually raised as live foods. Among the larger animals, the common crabs, shrimp, and lobsters, it is best to assume that they should be one-to-a-tank, as most are not very social, and many are markedly cannibalistic. Only the smallest species, of course, can be considered for a nano aquarium. A few deserve special mention, but you may find many potential specimens for your nano tank that are not named here.

Saltwater hermit crabs
(left and right).

Figure 8.1
Cleaner Shrimp

Lysmata amboinensis

L. debelius

L. grabhami

L. wurdemanni

Cleaner Shrimp

Cleaner shrimp of the genus *Lysmata* are popular. Each species is some variation of red and white. They also vary in sociability, and some are found naturally in groups, but cannibalism is always a possibility, especially if food and hiding places are scarce. Though they will clean parasites from fish, they are not obligate cleaners and will thrive even in systems without fish. Common names attached to these animals are fluid, and you can often find several species called by the same set of names. These crustaceans are increasingly available as tank-bred specimens.

Hardy, colorful, and personable, these shrimp are safe in any system that does not house animals large enough to eat them. Although there are occasional reports of predation on sessile invertebrates, the vast majority of reef tanks house some of them without incident. Like most other cleaners, they are bold, and it is common for them to congregate on an aquarist's submerged arm, busily poking around for possible tidbits.

Lysmata debelius, perhaps the deepest red of the group and often called the fire or blood shrimp because of this, would make a spectacular—if pricey—nano aquarium inhabitant. Still deep red, but with a skunk-like white dorsal stripe instead of white spots, *L. amboinensis* comes from the Indo-Pacific, but the very similar *L. grabhami* is found on both sides of the Atlantic. The least expensive of the group is *L. wurdemanni*, often called the peppermint shrimp because of its candy-cane striping (see Figure 8.1). This Caribbean species is highly sought after by aquarists plagued with *Aiptasia* anemones, since the shrimp will often feed on that pest. It can be kept successfully in small to large groups. A few related and very similar looking species are occasionally inadvertently brought in as contaminants.

Coral Banded Shrimp

Also known as boxer shrimp, these flamboyant red-, white-, and black-banded shrimp with extra-long antennae are popular and readily available. There are a few color variants of *Stenopus hispidus* as well as other species in the genus that are occasionally imported. These animals are highly territorial and will not tolerate other crustaceans, including conspecifics. They do, however, live naturally as mated pairs, and it is often possible to buy mated pairs that have been collected and shipped together. Mated pairs are much more likely to remain out and visible, as single individuals often hide among the rock.

Like the smaller *Lysmata* shrimp, these shrimp are facultative cleaners, though for some reason cleaning behavior that is commonly observed in the wild is rarely seen in captivity. They are greedy feeders and will eat just about anything, from fish foods to small sleeping fish. They are fairly adaptable as long as conditions remain stable, but they cannot tolerate any dissolved wastes, so filtration, especially biofiltration, is a priority.

So here is an animal that isn't safe around other invertebrates or small fish but is reef safe, not harming corals and other sessile inverts. It is colorful and has interesting behaviors, but in a large tank it may spend much of its time hidden in the live rock. Sounds perfect for a nano setup, doesn't it?

Stenopus hispidus

Painted, Harlequin, Clown Shrimp

The genus *Hymenocera* has several species that regularly appear in the hobby. Attractive and comical looking, these animals have a grisly side— they only eat starfish, and they normally eat them alive. They have been maintained with frozen starfish, but aquarists also keep them by supplying them with *Asterina*, those small starfish that often proliferate in mature systems. Sometimes welcome as scavengers, these small stars reproduce quickly and can reach plague

Hymenocera elegans (left)
H. picta (right)

proportions. If you have a system with a heavy *Asterina* population to provide food for them, you could consider a nano featuring a mated pair of *Hymenocera*, but otherwise you should forgo these fascinating but demanding shrimp.

Mollusks

Of the three major groups of mollusks (bivalves, gastropods, and cephalopods), only gastropods are generally appropriate for nano systems. Maintaining the filter-feeding bivalves is extremely problematic in small volumes, and cephalopods, even the smallest species, are simply too large and active for most nano tanks. Both shell-less nudibranchs and shelled snails can be considered, but the former are extremely limited in appropriateness.

Nudibranchs

It is natural poetic justice that the lowly garden slug has marine relatives that are among the most exotic and beautiful animals on our planet. Elaborate frills and flamboyant coloration mark many marine nudibranchs, or sea slugs. The largest (16 inches, 40 cm) is *Hexabranchus sanguineus*, known as the Spanish dancer because of its resemblance to the frilly dresses of flamenco dancers when it swims. As is often the case, the bright colors of many of these shell-less mollusks indicate that they are toxic. Such aposematic coloration warns off potential predators. Typically a nudibranch's toxins are taken from its prey and stored in its tissues. Although various nudibranchs are frequently seen in the trade, very few of them are suitable for an aquarium of any size and will not survive in captivity.

Berghia verrucicornis

This results from their extremely specialized diets. It is almost as if nudibranchs specialize in specialization. A species of nudibranch may prey on only a single species of invertebrate, but that might be a coral, hydroid, sponge, or even another species of nudibranch. As a group, sea slugs eat a huge variety of animals, but any particular nudibranch typically preys on an extremely restricted number of species.

There are two nudibranchs commonly touted as suitable for captivity, but both still have dietary problems, and their suitability for nano setups is even more questionable. The first is the genus *Berghia*. Although the aquarium animals are usually identified as *Berghia verrucicornis*, other species may also be involved. In any case, these attractive little nudibranchs are valued because they eat *Aiptasia* anemones—and only *Aiptasia* anemones. Aquarists plagued with an *Aiptasia* proliferation welcome these slugs into their tanks, but once the pests are eliminated, the nudibranchs will starve to death. A natural balance between predator and prey could theoretically result in tanks with a baseline population of both animals showing consecutive spikes and dips in numbers, but the artificial ecosystem of an aquarium will, in practice, not be balanced over the long term. Obviously, the small volume of a nano setup precludes even a very short-term balance.

Aiptasia anemones. The food item of choice of the nudibranch *Berghia verrucicornis*.

The other common aquarium sea slug is actually not a nudibranch, even though its common name is lettuce nudibranch. *Elysia* (*Tridachia*) *crispata* is in the order Sacoglossa (as opposed to Nudibranchia) and is an algae eater and is often sold to control nuisance algae. It is probably easier to establish a steady population of these slugs than it is with *Berghia* in a mature reef system, but it's not going to happen in a nano. Of course, if you can provide supplemental algae on a regular basis, it might be possible to maintain an *Elysia* slug in a nano system. The problem here again is that if the food source dries up, the animals cannot switch to other foods and will starve.

So why have we gone to such lengths to describe animals we are not recommending? Because these unsuitable animals are extremely common in the hobby, and even experienced aquarists often recommend the two latter species. We hope that by providing details about these invertebrates we will dissuade you from purchasing them inappropriately.

Figure 8.2

A Snail, a Conch, and a Star

A triton trumpet snail.

Strombus sp.

Linckia multiflora, a starfish that will do well in nano marine aquaria.

Snails

All of the snails commonly sold as detritivores or algae eaters for marine aquaria can be used in nano systems. From tiny sand-sifting snails to large *Trochus*, all popular snails will do well in a nano. It is important, however, to watch the food supply carefully. It is rare that an aquarist has to worry about feeding snails in a large system where there is plenty of food available, but a small system might not have enough "leftovers" for the snails, and you may have to provide food specifically for them.

Conchs

Various conchs of the genus *Strombus* are being commercially bred for the aquarium hobby, and they make interesting pets in appropriate systems—which do not include nano tanks. You could, of course focus on a juvenile specimen in your nano system and move it to a larger aquarium as it grows.

Echinoderms

Most commonly available starfish and urchins are too large for all but the largest nano setups. Various burrowing stars, however, are ideally suited, both because of their diminutive size and because of their detritivorous habits. You can purchase these tiny stars, but they also often arrive in live rock or sand. Here is yet another case where a nano setup gives you the opportunity to observe organisms that would otherwise be overlooked (see Figure 8.2).

Sessile Inverts

Many popular reef animals can at least theoretically be kept in nano setups. The theoretical part goes back to the caution that it is much more difficult to maintain pristine water conditions in small volumes. That aside, most species are suitable for nanos, with obvious exceptions like giant clams and large coral colonies. Colonial inverts and those that reproduce asexually can outgrow the room allotted to them, even in a large aquarium, but they can be divided and moved to other systems. In fact, a nano is a great place to enjoy a small coral colony that would be overlooked in a large reef tank. At some point you can move it to a larger setup, replacing it with a new specimen or a frag from the old one.

Sponges

Sponges are not commonly kept, even in large setups. Their filter feeding is a major obstacle and would be even more of a problem in a nano setup. Most surviving sponges arrive with live rock and by definition are adaptable to aquarium conditions. It could happen in a nano tank, but it is unlikely, and adding a sponge intentionally to a nano system is a bad idea.

Cnidarians

The various polyps, anemones, and corals that are the Cnidaria are the focus of the reef hobby. It was the breakthroughs in the keeping of these animals that made a reef aquarium possible. The current state of the art is that it is possible to maintain a closed marine system with such precision that aquarists can create the pristine conditions required by reef invertebrates in very small aquaria. It is best to master the basics of reef husbandry on a large setup, but once you are comfortable with monitoring and maintaining the complex chemistry of a reef system, you can try to go nano (see Figure 8.3).

Of course, there are ways to have a nano reef with a bit less effort. The pest glass anemone of the genus *Aiptasia* are as bulletproof as a marine invertebrate can be. A bit touchier but still fairly hardy are zoanthids and other polyps. A few select pieces of live rock and a colony or two of these cnidarians can make a spectacular display that, while still sensitive, will not require the absolute precision that a system with stony corals will. They are also less demanding in terms of light intensity.

A Cautionary Note

Very small—even tiny—reef tanks are possible. Small-polyp stony corals can be kept in extremely small volumes. Very few first-time hobbyists, however, can maintain these animals, even in 150-gallon (600-liter) tanks. It is decidedly more likely that you will succeed with a nano reef setup if you first become proficient at keeping corals in a large system. If you choose to make a nano tank your first reef, enlist the aid of an experienced reef aquarist who can guide you step by step.

Specimen Display

We've already touched on many possibilities for specimen tanks, such as shrimp individuals or pairs. A beautiful display can also be made with a single coral colony on a few pieces of live rock rubble.

Figure 8.3

Corals

All photographs showcase specimens from a 24-gallon (96-liter) tank.

Blue-green Florida ricordia mushroom coral, *Ricordea florida.*

Xenia sp.

Frogspawn coral, *Euphyllia paradivisa.*

Sun coral, *Tubastraea* sp.

Blue zoanthids, *Zoanthidea* sp.

Orange short tentacle plate coral, *Fungia* sp.

Clove polyps, *Clavularia* sp.

Toadstool leather coral, *Sarcophyton* sp.

Community Display

As we mentioned in the previous chapter regarding fish, the size of a nano severely restricts any possible communities. Invertebrates, however, present much less of a bioload than do fish. In addition many fish specimen displays can be invertebrate communities! In fact, a nano reef with just one small fish but several corals is a great idea.

Biotope Display

As with fish, a tidepool display is an option for a biotope setup. A nano focus could be used in a Caribbean biotope with Florida aquacultured live rock and several peppermint shrimp. A small damsel or other Caribbean fish could complete the system.

Neopetrolisthes sp. A single crab is just one more example of a marine invertebrate nano specimen display.

A nano tank is a relitively inexpensive alternative to keeping a massive reef tank. Here, a colony of mushroom coral *Actinodiscus* sp. lives contently in a 14-gallon (96-liter) tank

Vivaria

Chapter **9**

Definitions

The terms for glass-enclosed microcosms all stem from the *aquarium*, a glass vessel of water as a home for aquatic organisms. By analogy, a *terrarium* is a glass vessel with a soil substrate and planted with terrestrial plants. Often when it includes terrestrial animals as well, it is called a *vivarium*, which technically is a glass vessel containing living things. The term *paludarium*, from the Latin root *palud-* meaning "swamp," is used for vessels containing both aquatic and terrestrial sections, each with appropriate plants and animals.

We cannot forget the desktop vivarium—a terrarium or paludarium that houses terrestrial plants and animals. These terms are partially interchangeable, and the distinctions among them are easily blurred. You could have a small "stream" in a terrarium, but if you increase the size of the stream, many would say you have a paludarium. Any container with plants and animals in it could be considered a vivarium. But no matter what you call it, the nano concept can be applied to this type of system.

Historical Considerations

The history of nano vivaria is quite parallel to that of nano aquaria. For a long time, most terraria and vivaria were on the small side—desktop greenhouses in effect, but as the herptile hobby expanded and the availability of reptile and amphibian species burgeoned, people started using larger and larger enclosures. Many hobbyists would dedicate entire rooms in their homes to their reptiles as they started to keep 5-foot (1.5-m) iguanas and even larger monitors and pythons.

Keeping vivaria started with herps like iguanas, and the hobby has blossomed since, expanding to frogs, snakes, and insects.

Figure 9.1

Dwarf Chameleons

The diminutive dwarf chameleons almost require a nano setup. In anything larger than a desktop terrarium they will be lost to sight.

Brookesia sp.

Rhampholeon brevicaudatus

Figure 9.2

Dwarf Chameleons and Geckoes

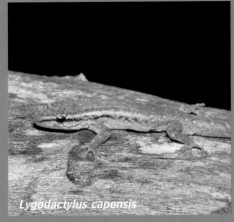

Lygodactylus capensis

Rhampholeon sp. "stumpfi"

Brookesia sp.

L. luteopicturatus

Lygodactylus sp.

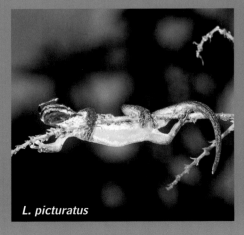

L. picturatus

R. brevicaudatus

Many herpers cannot look at an aquarium without thinking what sort of reptile cage it would make, so desktop aquaria got some of them thinking nano—about small vivaria with the smallest of herps in them. The currently popular dwarf chameleons in the genera *Brookesia* and *Rhampholeon* (see Figure 9.1) are perfect for a nano system. In a large vivarium they would be lost—or eaten—but in a tiny tank they are almost always visible, even if they are hiding in the leaf litter. Likewise for dwarf geckoes in the genus *Lygodactylus*, which are diurnal and very personable, but easily lost or eaten in a large vivarium (see Figure 9.2).

The Problem of Water

Since this is a book about aquaria, it makes sense to concentrate on the paludarium, in which fish can be part of the setup. Whether or not fish are present, water is a considerable factor in any vivarium, and the smaller the vivarium, the greater the concern. Fungus and mold often flourish in poorly designed systems, and the balance between moist and soggy is difficult to maintain. While desert terraria—and nano desert terraria—are certainly possible, when water is present in more than just a small bowl, the resultant paludarium mandates a high-humidity environment. The plants and animals included therefore have to be those that thrive under moist conditions.

Air Flow

Circulation of air through the enclosure is important in preventing condensation and moldy conditions. Often a wire mesh top is insufficient in providing enough air flow. Reptile cages made of soft screening are available, but they are not watertight. They can be adapted with a watertight basin as the bottom for a paludarium with excellent ventilation. If all the plants and animals are from tropical rainforest jungles and streams, high humidity is good, but the soil must be well drained to prevent mold.

False Bottoms

One of the standard solutions to the problem of draining the soil is to build the vivarium with a false bottom. A divider (screen, plastic mesh, or even an old undergravel filter plate) is raised with short lengths of PVC pipe to provide an inch or so (a few centimeters) of clearance on the bottom of the aquarium, then the soil is placed on top of the divider. Excess water drains into this space, preventing the soil from becoming waterlogged.

This photograph illustrates a lightweight expanded clay aggregate (LECA) false bottom, currently a popular choice in vivarium building. It's very porous, helping with drainage, and plants can root easily in it.

If the goal is a paludarium with a pond area, the divider covers only the land portion of the tank, and a mesh or grid prevents animals from entering the reservoir under the soil. Such a design necessitates a very shallow pond, but this can be overcome with a tiered setup.

Tiers

One way of keeping terrestrial plant roots from rotting in water-saturated soil is to create a tiered design. The lowest tier consists of the water and adjacent "shore," then one or more tiers are built up using retaining walls of stone or wood. Since water seeks its own level, the water "table" in the soil will be at the same height as the surface of the pond or stream area. While higher soil may be quite moist, it will not have standing water in it.

Substrate

Garden soil is used in many vivaria, often with a layer of gravel under it to improve drainage. Unless you are certain the soil does not have any fertilizers or pesticides in it, you should not use it in a system that will include animals of any kind. In many cases, gravel or sand is a better choice. The plants can often be planted right in the gravel, especially if the gravel bed is only slightly higher than the water level and the plants are bog species—their roots will be under water. To keep terrestrial plants, or if you want to have the gravel considerably higher than the water level, the plants can be in pots. The soil in the pots should stay moist from capillary action, but it is a simple matter to water the pots during a water change if they need it.

Filtration?

Filtration is a problem in any paludarium, but a nano system presents even more difficulties. One viable option is to use undergravel filter technology, turning the "land"

Leaves, soil, and rocks can make up a substrate that some frogs and insects will thrive in.

portion of the vessel into the filter. The substrate should be gravel for best results.

A small water pump and some tubing are the only equipment needed. If it can be hidden in the aquascaping, the pump can be submersible. Otherwise, a siphon tube should run from the water to the pump, which can be situated under the tank or otherwise out of sight. In either case, the output of the pump is directed through tubing to a high point in the land section. The water will percolate down through the gravel and back into the pond area. This way the entire gravel bed is being used as a biofilter. The pumps designed for small fountains can often be used in such a setup.

Lighting

Terrestrial plants require much less intense lighting than aquatic plants, since the light does not have to penetrate water to reach the plants. In many cases a standard aquarium fluorescent fixture will provide sufficient light, but the popularity of nano freshwater planted and nano reef tanks ensures the availability of higher-intensity choices.

Figure 9.3
Plants

Echinodorus tenellus

Myriophyllum aquaticum

Cryptocoryne beckettii

Taxiphyllum barbieri

Decor

Rocks, vines, and driftwood can be used as ornaments. They can also serve as hiding and breeding places for paludarium inhabitants. It can, however, be difficult to keep mold from growing on vines and wood. A properly lit and ventilated vivarium should not have mold problems, but it is often possible to keep the vessel mold-free without wood but not with it. The smaller the system, the more likely that humidity problems will present themselves.

Plants

While many plants can be trimmed and pruned to fit into a very small tank, to avoid a crowded appearance and thereby implement the nano focus, you need to choose nano plants. These include truly dwarf specimens like miniature African violets, but overall size is not as much of a concern as is leaf size. For example, the creeping fig vine *Ficus pumila* is a plant that will climb all the way up tall tree trunks, but its tiny leaves put it on a perfect scale for a nano system. As the vine grows, it can be clipped back to remain tidy, but the 2-cm (less than an inch) heart-shaped leaves give the impression of an exotic jungle vine in miniature.

Many popular aquarium plants can be used in a paludarium, where they will grow emersed leaves above the water line. These include popular swordplants, genus *Echinodorus*, parrot's feather, *Myriophyllum aquaticum*, and many other stem plants. Often such plants will grow up out of the water and onto the "shore," continuing to spread across moist soil.

Some aquarium plants will actually thrive under bog conditions completely out of the water as long as they are wet. These include many *Cryptocoryne* species, Java fern, *Microsorum pteropus,* and Java moss, *Taxiphyllum barbieri* (*Vesicularia dubyana*).

Still other species commonly sold for aquarium use are actually bog plants—terrestrials that like to grow with their roots under water. While these plants may survive and even grow when completely submerged, they will positively thrive when kept in more natural conditions. These plants include (see Figure 9.3):

- Purple waffle plant, *Hemigraphis colorata* var. "exotica"
- Brazilian sword or peace lily, *Spathiophyllum*

- Japanese fan plants, genus *Acorus*
- Arrowheads, genus *Syngonium*
- Mondo grasses, genus *Ophiopogon*

Moss

A common mistake paludarium keepers make is to collect local mosses for their display. Temperate mosses will not survive in a typical paludarium. They simply cannot handle the sustained high temperatures, and often the setup is too wet for them, even given that they occur in moist places. Fortunately, it is possible to buy various tropical species of moss that will thrive in a tropical rainforest paludarium—since their natural habitat is a tropical rainforest! They will happily spread across the substrate in low-light areas.

Dish Bogs and Ponds

We began this chapter with the observation that it is not always possible to pigeonhole a setup, as there aren't distinct boundaries between terrarium and paludarium, between paludarium and vivarium. For example, the plants in a paludarium can grow not only out of the water but also out of the vessel, pushing high above the glass sides. At some point you'd probably consider the display to be a collection of specimens planted in an aquarium rather than a pot.

Well, instead imagine the glass sides of the paludarium shrinking down, leaving more and more of the plants exposed to the room. Soon you'd have the equivalent of a dish paludarium, like the popular dish garden. And dish bog gardens, or even dish "ponds," are a possible application of the nano concept. In fact, desktop water features have become quite popular, though in most cases they include neither plants nor animals—desktop fountains and waterfalls are used both for their beauty and for the soothing sound of running water.

Plants can be used in dish bogs and ponds, but terrestrial animals are obviously out—literally, since they would quickly

Figure 9.3 (continued)

Hemigraphis sp.

Acorus pusillus

Ophiopogon japonicus

leave the dish for your draperies or sofa. If the sides of the container are sufficiently high above the water surface, you could consider some tiny fish, but do not underestimate their ability to jump!

Vivarium Vertebrates

Various vertebrate animals can be used in a nano vivarium. One of the major concerns here is airflow. Even animals that require high humidity will not tolerate overly damp conditions, which lead to respiratory infections. If there is condensation on the glass walls of the vivarium, there is probably insufficient airflow. As discussed earlier, a screen top may be sufficient to deal with the moisture, but it may not be. One alternative is to have a small fan blowing across the screen top to pull the water vapor out of the vivarium.

Mudskippers (family Gobiidae, subfamily Oxudercinae) have distinct features that leave little doubt to observers what they are. The only problem, as it is with any group of fishes, is distinguishing between species. It is important to know exactly which mudskipper you are purchasing, as some can grow in excess of 7 inches (18 cm), a length that exceeds the maximum for nano aquaria.

Fish

Of course, if you select fish rather than reptiles for your vivarium, excess humidity ceases to be a concern. Any fish suitable for a nano aquarium can be used in a nano paludarium, but certain fish are especially well suited. Topping the list has to be the mudskipper—a fish that spends most of its time on land. Mudskippers require not only high humidity but also high air temperature, so a tightly fitting glass top is important. This—and the fact that they are brackish fishes that require some salt in their water—dictates an unplanted vivarium in most cases, though small mangroves will thrive with their roots in brackish water. See "Biotope Display" at the end of this chapter for details.

Amphibians

To the dwarf frogs and newts we discussed in connection with nano tanks in Chapter 5 we can add for the vivarium small terrestrial frogs like tree, walking, reed, and poison dart frogs (see Figure 9.4). Small terrestrial salamanders are also suitable, though their cryptic lifestyle will render them effectively invisible most of the time. For a very small vivarium consider the squirrel frog, *Hyla squirella,* which tops out at 20 to 40 mm (up to an inch and a half) but is usually seen smaller. The partially aquatic fire-bellied toads of the genus *Bombina* will liven up a paludarium with their colors and their energetic—for an anuran —habits.

Hyla squirella

These terrestrial amphibians will require live foods—worms or insects. You must be very careful not to overcrowd these animals. Aside from potential aggression issues, you have to consider the mess they produce. The wastes from even one or two small frogs can quickly become an aesthetic and hygienic concern in a small enclosure.

Another problem many people are unprepared for is the predatory nature of most amphibians. They can and will swallow any other animal that they can, and in the case of frogs, that is often an animal almost the same size as they are—and length is not the only consideration, since a long, thin animal can be curled around in the predator's gut. A 3-inch (8-cm) tree frog can easily consume a 5-inch (12-cm) anole. Species does not matter at all, and frogs will eagerly ingest smaller specimens of their own species, so specimens must all be of the same size.

As mentioned, most caecilians are terrestrial; they burrow in moist soil. Again, however, adult size precludes keeping them in nano terraria, but a juvenile could be a temporary—though rarely seen—nano resident.

Figure 9.4

Frogs

Genus Key
Fire-bellied toads – *Bombina* spp.
Poison dart frogs – *Dendrobates* spp.
Reed frogs – *Heterixalus* spp.
Tree frogs – *Litoria, Pachymedusa, and Phyllomedusa* spp.
Walking frogs – *Kassina* spp.

D. lehmanni

Bombina bombina

B. variegatus

D. tinctorius

B. orientalis

Dendrobates auratus

Heterixalus alboguttatus

H. alboguttatus

Kassina maculata

Litoria caerulea

H. cf. betsileo

K. senegalensis

Pachymedusa dacnicolor

H. madagascariensis

K. weali

Phyllomedusa tomopterna

201

Diadophis sp.

Reptiles

We've already mentioned dwarf chameleons and geckos as ideal nano vivarium inhabitants. An anole or two (never two males!) will add activity to the foliage. The tiniest of snakes are possible specimens, but feeding them can be problematic, and you must make sure to choose a species that will thrive in a moist environment. Juvenile ring snakes, genus *Diadophis*, are a possibility.

A special consideration for vivarium reptiles is that many require special lighting that provides the UV radiation they need. In addition, reptiles require a basking spot where they can raise their body temperature for proper digestion of their food. In many nano setups the regular lighting may provide enough heat if a branch or other perch can get the animal close enough. You should discuss your desired setup with the person from who you are getting the reptile to make sure that you will be providing the proper environment.

Turtles?

Though banned from a nano aquarium, a turtle hatchling could work in a nano paludarium that is on the large side, but I still cannot recommend it. Turtles will trample or eat vegetation, and they can dig up substrates just by moving over them. In addition, they produce copious wastes. They can make wonderful aquarium or paludarium specimens, but only in sufficiently large habitats that are designed with their special needs in mind, not in nano setups.

Other Vertebrates?

No mammals are suitable for vivaria, and birds can only be considered for truly gargantuan, walk-through vivaria. They simply have no place in any nano system.

Invertebrates for the Vivarium

Invertebrates like beetles, earthworms, and isopods (sow bugs, pill bugs) may arrive with the soil or the plants, and some hobbyists add them. These animals, if they establish themselves, act as a cleanup crew, scavenging organic material. Various other invertebrates can be included in a vivarium for ornament and interest.

Crawling Critters

Millipedes, mantids, twig insects, and roaches are just some of the "bugs" kept as "pets" that will thrive in an appropriate vivarium (see Figure 9.5). Many of these animals are highly predatory, so compatibility issues are important to consider. Walking sticks require specialized plant diets and may be difficult to feed year-round. Tarantulas and other arachnids, including scorpions, are also popular nowadays, but they are normally kept in more arid vivaria, not moist terraria or paludaria.

Other Inverts

Land hermit crabs are suitable for many vivaria. They are also called tree crabs and will climb around in the vegetation. These terrestrial crabs have a soft abdomen that they place into a discarded shell. As they grow, the crabs need to find larger shells to move into. Despite the "hermit" part of their name, they are gregarious and do best in groups. They can be fed a wide variety of plant and animal foods and will scavenge as well. These crabs need access to both fresh and brackish water (a small dish will suffice), but they will drown if they fall into a pond area and cannot get out. Because of their size, they are of limited usefulness for nano systems, but small specimens may work in larger nanos.

Land snails of many species make interesting vivarium inhabitants. Many are small, and their overall lack of activity means they will adapt well to nano vivaria. Two cautions regarding terrestrial snails: they may be illegal to keep, so you should check local laws, and they may decimate any plantings you have in your vivarium (which is why they are illegal in some places). Feeding snails soft foods like mushrooms or lettuce may help keep them from sampling your plants, but it is best to consider a plantless

Figure 9.5

Crawling Critters

Earthworms

Beetle

Millipede

Walking stick

Hermit crabs naturally love to climb, so including small obstacles in their tank is much appreciated!

Moths (left) and butterflies (right) can kept in a vivarium, but doing so may be quite a challenge.

setup for snails. It is common for snails to lay eggs and successfully reproduce in captivity. The tiny snails that hatch out feed readily on soft plants.

Lepidoptera

With close to 200,000 species, the order Lepidoptera (butterflies and moths) is sure to have at least one suitable for just about any setup. These animals have had a marginal but persistent presence in the pet hobby. The larvae (caterpillars) often feed exclusively on one type of plant, and the adults are typically short-lived and delicate. Still, if their needs can be met, a butterfly or two can make a fascinating and educational addition to a desktop vivarium.

Specimen Display

Most fish can be kept without any regard to their natural biotope, and their needs can be met with just about any setup in terms of planting, decor, substrate, etc. This is not the case for the fish best suited to a vivarium or paludarium system: mudskippers. They

cannot survive in a regular aquarium and need the setup to imitate many aspects of their natural environment. Thus, the ideal vivarium fish display is also a biotope display.

Community Display

A vivarium gives the unique opportunity to make a community of aquatic, semi-aquatic, and terrestrial organisms. A nano paludarium could include aquatic plants, floating plants, bog plants, and fully terrestrial plants, as well as a newt, a few fish, and a tree frog. The possibilities are endless and limited mainly by the size and design of your system.

Although many paludaria are divided into left and right sections, a popular variant is to divide the tank front to back, leaving the rear for land and the front half for water. With such a design it is easy to produce a river- or stream-like setup. A couple of barriers of different height can divide the "stream," providing waterfalls. The planted land area can either go straight to the bottom of the tank, or it can be raised above the water level, leaving the entire bottom of the aquarium as part of the water section. This undercut stream bed design maximizes the number of fish you can keep and provides an especially natural look.

Agalychnis callidryas, the red-eyed tree frog, an uncommon but beautiful specimen.

Biotope Display

A wonderful nano biotope is a mudskipper mud flat, although hygiene concerns dictate that you forgo the mud for sand or gravel. You will need to use one of the smaller mudskipper species like *Periophthalmus modestus, P. novemradiatus,* or the new "Indian mudskipper," all about 100 mm (4 inches), and you should not try to keep more than one in the tank. If you use a reef-tank definition of "nano" and have a 30- or 40-gallon (120- or

Periophthalmus novemradiatus

160-liter) system, you can try a small group as long as only one male is included, but serious aggression is always a possibility with these unusual gobies.

At least half the tank bottom area should be "land," with sand being an ideal substrate. A horizontal piece of driftwood and/or some small rocks will provide places for the fish to climb around. The water need only be deep enough to allow the fish to submerge completely; it will spend little time in the water. Mudskippers can thrive in full-salinity sea water or brackish water down to about half salinity. Although they will not immediately drop dead if placed into fresh water, they will not do well or live long in it. Marine salt mix, not plain sodium chloride, must be used to provide the proper water chemistry, especially with regard to pH and alkalinity.

If the vessel is tall enough, you can plant a couple of mangrove propagules either in the land portion or, if the substrate there is deep enough, in the water area. Mangroves can be planted with their roots in water or in moist soil. You will need to provide adequate light for the mangroves, but an unplanted mudskipper system only needs whatever light you require to enjoy watching it.

Biofiltration is very important, as mudskippers cannot tolerate ammonia and nitrite. In addition, frequent—even daily—water changes are required. A submersible heater in the water section and a complete lid should keep the humidity and air temperature high enough. Although mudskippers can usually be trained to take non-living foods once they associate their keepers with mealtime, they will need live foods like worms and crickets at least at first.

Tankmates are problematic. Most vivarium animals cannot tolerate brackish conditions, and any that could would likely either eat your mudskipper or be eaten by it. Peaceful fish too small to be swallowed—do not underestimate the size of a mudskipper's mouth!—will probably be ignored by the mudskipper, but aggressive fish could keep it from returning to the water, in which case it will not survive. The real problem, however, is that the typical setup for amphibious mudskippers is not generally friendly toward fish. In a large paludarium in which the shore descends into water a foot (30 cm) deep or more, various brackish-water fish would be possible tankmates, but a nano system is unlikely to have water more than a couple of inches (5 cm) deep.

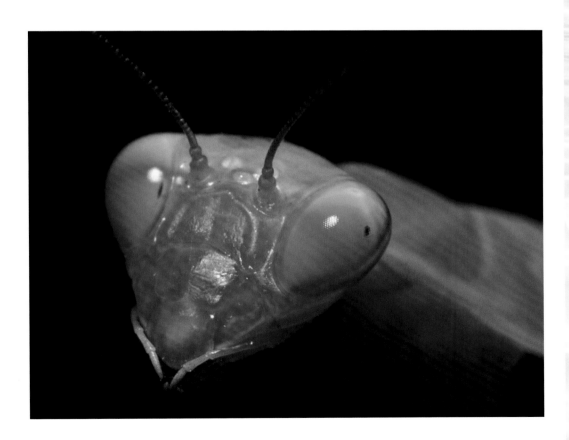

Ponds

Chapter 10

We've already looked at desktop ponds, but the nano concept can be applied to outdoor garden ponds as well. In fact, it developed independently of the desktop aquarium concept, as container ponds have been popular for quite some time. As with aquaria, the nano concept works when the focus of the pond is microcosmic—a bucket with a water lily, a few cattails, and several goldfish is a crowded mess, a result of trying to stuff regular pond specimens into a bucket. On the other hand, a single dwarf reed, some frogbit, and a group of *Heterandria formosa* turn the same bucket into a nano pond, with the same sense of art, relaxation, and natural microcosm as a large in-ground setup.

Half whiskey barrels are perfect as a container for your nano pond, but containers come in all shapes, sizes, and types, including concrete and plastic. Just as with an aquarium you keep inside your home, only your imagination is the limit!

Container

Often the container for a container pond is as important as the inhabitants. Half whiskey barrels have long been used for water gardens, and preformed plastic liners are available to fit them. Large glazed or plastic flowerpots and urns also make great nano ponds. Although ponds are traditionally opaque, viewed only from above, transparent vessels can be used for aquatic gardens, marrying the nano pond with the aquarium. In fact, many aquarists locate aquaria outside on the deck or in the yard during the summer, and some take advantage of this opportunity to grow emergent and floating pond plants.

Planting

Remember to keep the bonsai principle in mind—the goal is a miniature water garden with the same sense of balance and proportion as a large pond, only in scale with the container size. Dwarf lilies can replace regular water lilies in larger nano ponds, but for even smaller setups, try one of the aquarium lilies or even frogbit. The popular "banana plant" is actually a relative of water lilies and makes a similar display in tiny ponds.

Aquarists are often flabbergasted by the growth of pond plants. Intense summer sunlight can be approximated by extremely high intensity lighting, but if you've never used that, the speed at which plants grow outdoors will surprise you. Anacharis *Egeria densa* and *Cabomba* will both quickly grow several feet, trailing across the water and sporting small white flowers. Duckweed will cover a pond seemingly overnight. Of course, pruning in a nano pond is not much of a chore, and the cuttings can often be used to plant other ponds or aquariums.

Pond keepers typically choose between hardy plants that will withstand winter's freeze and tropical plants that must be overwintered indoors or replaced each spring. Because nano ponds have small volumes and are usually above ground, they may freeze too completely for even hardy plants to survive. It should be possible, however, to move a nano pond to a sheltered location like a garage or basement where the plants can go through dormancy. You can also plant a nano pond with tropical plants and then bring it indoors in the fall and keep it under a high intensity light until it can go back out in the spring. Most nano ponds can be moved simply by emptying the water, moving the pond, then refilling. You can leave a very small amount of water in it during transport so you don't have to remove the fish.

Flowering *Egeria densa*.

Although many people prefer a portable setup for container ponds, such a nano system can be installed permanently where garden space is limited, allowing even postage-stamp gardens to have a built-in water feature. Marginal plants that are usually planted in pond shallows can be adapted to a nano setup in several ways without taking up valuable pond space.

You can simply plant marginals in rich soil around the pond and water them daily to keep the soil wet. An alternative is to dig out the area for marginal plantings and line it with a pond liner before filling it back in. This makes essentially a pond full of dirt, and it will hold water to keep the soil wet. Using a flexible liner, this marginal area can be any shape at all—even serpentine, curving around the pond itself. Dwarf versions of rushes, papyrus, bamboo, and cattails, along with low-growing marginals, will keep the planting from overwhelming the tiny pond.

While a large garden pond might have a cascade feature built of boulders and flowing

Most nano ponds do not utilize filtration, but using it cannot hurt your setup.

into the pond basin, the micro version could be a tiny waterfall over a cluster of rocks. This would provide aeration and aesthetics on a bonsai scale.

Filtration

Garden ponds tend to be underfiltered, which is unfortunate, since there are many effective pond filters on the market. Koi keepers are probably the most likely to use filtration, but even the smallest koi are absolutely out of the question for a nano setup.

People think of garden ponds as miniature versions of natural ponds and lakes, which don't have any filters. They do, however, have filtration! In addition to the nitrifying biofiltration we are familiar with in our aquaria, natural bodies of water have denitrifying biofiltration and filtration by vegetation. Bacteria in muddy sediments convert nitrate into nitrogen and oxygen, and growing plants remove large quantities of ammonia and phosphate from the water. Most natural ponds have water changes, too, either from springs or other water flow, or from rain and overflow.

So, can you get by in a nano pond with heavy planting and plenty of water changes? Sure, and that is probably the easiest way to go. Adapting a regular pond filter to a nano pond will have the same problems—such as creating a whirlpool—as using a regular aquarium filter on a nano tank. You may also, however, have the option of adapting a regular aquarium filter to your nano pond; canister filters in particular could be quite suitable. But if you want to take the water change route, it is especially easy to change water outside, either draining it onto the ground or even using the water to water flower baskets (which often need daily watering in the summer).

Figure 10.1

Native Fish

American hobbyists are just now discovering the desirability of many native fish for their aquaria, but U.S. natives have been popular among European aquarists for a long time.

Heterandria formosa

Jordanella floridae

Fish Selection

Almost any aquarium fish can be put into a nano pond. Even fish banned by size from the nano tank may be suitable for a container pond. Don't overdo it, though! Keep the bonsai principle in mind, and remember that whatever species you choose, they have to be able to handle the temperature fluctuations that take place in a nano pond.

Native Fish

Obviously fish native to temperate regions, especially those found in shallow water habitats (usually the best aquarium choices), are well adapted to the conditions of a nano pond. *Heterandria formosa* is the smallest poeciliid and suitable for the tiniest container pond (see Figure 10.1). Native killies are also great for nano ponds. The popular pupfish *Jordanella floridae*, known as the American flagfish, does very well in a mini pond. Larger fish like shiners and sunfish are best avoided. Riffle-dwelling species like many darters and dace may be small enough but require high oxygen levels that are hard to obtain in a small vessel of unmoving, warm water.

Summer Vacation

The summers in most temperate regions feature weather as hot as or hotter than that found in tropical climes, and many aquarists take advantage of the couple of months of tropical temperatures to give their fish an outdoor summer vacation.

Don't be fooled by the small, relatively inexpensive koi you may find for sale at a pet store. They are juveniles; mature koi, given enough space and good water quality, can grow to more than 3 feet (90 cm) in length! Koi should only be kept in large, deep ponds.

Figure 10.2

"Bonsai Koi"

Many of the different varieties of *Carassius auratus* give the appearance of koi keeping without the required backyard-swallowing ponds.

Sarassa

Shubunkin

Comet

"Bonsai Koi"

It is common to find a gardener who, excited about the idea of a pond, picks up a preformed pond at the local garden center. Once it is installed, the gardener buys some koi to stock it. Unfortunately, this is a horrible situation, doomed to failure. A koi pond should be at least 4 feet (120 cm) deep, preferably more, but these ponds are hardly half that. In addition, the overall dimensions of a proper koi pond are greater than many people's entire gardens! An ideal koi pond has a minimum of 250 gallons (950 liters) *per fish*, but most of these manufactured ponds hold less than half that. In addition, the massive filtration demanded by these huge fish is simply unavailable for small setups.

On the other hand, applying the nano principle to a koi pond, you can utilize many preformed garden ponds as goldfish ponds. Shubunkin, comet, and sarassa goldfish (see Figure 10.2) suggest koi both in coloration and in form, and in a pond they produce a similar effect on a much smaller scale. Fully grown goldfish are too large for most ponds that could be called nano, but after a summer as bonsai koi, they can be moved to larger ponds and replaced by new juveniles the next year.

Other Goldfish

Fancy goldfish varieties cannot be overwintered outside in many areas, but they can enjoy pond life during the milder parts of the year. It is especially important not to overcrowd these less-hardy strains, so you should figure at least 20 gallons (80 liters) per fish. If the fish are small, you can get by with a bit less. While this restricts their usage to larger nano systems, a single oranda or ryukin could make a stunning centerpiece in the right setup. Once again, you can stock your nano pond with juvenile goldfish and replace them each year, moving the old stock to larger quarters. Varieties like the celestial, originally bred to be viewed from above, will display very well in an adequately large system.

The eyes of a celestial goldfish are very delicate. If keeping one do not place anything in the pond with sharp or rough edges, as they can damage the delicate eye tissue.

Other Animals

Most typical pond animals other than fish and snails are unsuitable for nano systems. Besides being small fish predators, turtles and frogs will not stay in a nano pond. Newts are almost certain to wander away, too. Tadpoles are a possibility, but if you do not remove them late in metamorphosis, they too will hop away. Even crayfish will most likely disappear quickly.

The small completely aquatic invertebrates we discussed for freshwater nano aquaria in Chapter 6 are suitable for a pond as well, and some of them—particularly the insects—may show up uninvited.

Special Considerations

As with aquaria, some aspects of pondkeeping are magnified in nano ponds, while others are minimized. A water change on a pond can be a long and laborious undertaking, but it is a simple and rapid chore on a nano pond. Likewise, keeping plants trimmed and divided and repotted might be a continuous summer task for a regular garden pond, but a balcony water garden could be kept in perfect trim with only a few minutes' work on a few occasions. On the other hand, some concerns tend to be minor for most ponds, but extremely important for nano systems.

Temperature Regulation

On a languid dog-day afternoon, the water temperature in the shallows of a garden pond might be too hot to comfortably dip your toes, but your fish will be taking it easy under an awning of water lily leaves or near the bottom in the cool depths. A storm front passing through near sunset might drop the air temperature more than 30 degrees Fahrenheit (a drop of more than 20 degrees Celsius), plunging the shallows into the chilly range, but the fish will not notice much difference in the depths.

A container pond on the same afternoon could easily become a stewpot for the livestock. Were any to survive, they'd be chilled through during the night. If the absolute temperatures did not do them in, the repeated swings from one extreme to the other would. If the pond is buried in the ground, there would be much less of a problem, since most of its surface area will be insulated by the vast mass of earth. Container ponds, however, are almost always above-ground setups.

A pond built into the ground will help keep your fish from being boiled alive from the sunlight.

Stratification

In sunny weather, an unshaded pond without filter, waterfall, fountain, or other source of water movement will have significant temperature stratification. The top few inches might be in the 90s Fahrenheit (above 33°C), while at the bottom the temperature might be only 65°F (18°C). This situation also obtains in natural bodies of water, and fish can seek out the level at which they are most comfortable.

The same stratification will happen in a nano pond, provided it is deep enough so that the sun's rays do not penetrate to the bottom at full intensity. Thus, deep containers, even when they are not very large, are preferable for outdoor nano ponds. Providing shade for the pond will also help prevent dangerous overheating of the water.

Even a full covering of floating plants would, besides completely blocking your view of the pond, be inadequate to shade the nano pond. It is therefore important to locate a container water garden in the shade, or at least where it will be shaded during the hottest part of the day. Often this can be accomplished by placing it right up against an outside wall of the house, in the house's shadow. If your pond is on your deck or patio and you have an awning, that should do the trick.

Of course, the same thing that causes this problem—the enormous surface area relative to volume—also offers possible solutions. For example, an electric fan can be positioned to blow directly on the pond, greatly cooling it both by taking heat away from the sides of the container and by increasing the evaporation of water from the surface. In fact, you can combine both these ameliorative factors further by also spraying the sides of the container with water. As the fan evaporates this water, it will further cool the vessel.

Even a very small fountain will greatly aid a nano pond, providing aeration, water movement, and cooling. There are many small submersible pump and fountain setups that are plug-and-play, needing no additional plumbing.

Predator Control

While in some areas predation can be a major concern even for small lakes, most garden ponds have minimal losses and are adequately protected by placement near dwellings, some dense plantings, and a deep central area into which fish can flee from uninvited bird or mammal visitors. Still, garden ponds are sometimes decimated by predators, and a single predator could easily eliminate all the fish in a nano pond in a matter of seconds.

Probably the most dangerous animal for ponds of all sizes is the raccoon *Procyon lotor*. This merciless predator loves water and does not mind getting wet. It is also a messy plunderer, and a pond after a visit from a raccoon may have all of its plants uprooted and shredded as well as all of its fish killed. Since this mammal is often more numerous in suburban and urban locales than in rural, any pond keeper can suffer its predation. An accomplished climber, the raccoon can easily visit a balcony far above the ground, and fences offer no protection. Fortunately, their predations are nocturnal, which gives you the option of covering your nano pond at night. Since these animals are extremely dexterous and love to manipulate things with their hands—okay, front paws, but they use them like hands—covering the pond with netting will probably not deter them. A heavy board completely covering the container and weighted down with a few stones or bricks should do the trick. If you have plants growing out of the water, you might have to get more creative if raccoons are in your vicinity.

A domestic cat that is at most a nuisance to fish in a garden pond can manage to catch fish in a sufficiently small nano pond. However, cats detest getting wet and are usually fairly easy to chase off, so a little supervision should be sufficient to protect most ponds from feline predations.

Raccoons and cats are two animals you have to be mindful of when setting up a nano pond. Both have the ability—and desire—to eat whatever fishes you may be keeping in your pond.

Fish-eating birds like herons are unlikely to visit a nano pond, and the frogs, snakes, and turtles that can move into a garden pond and dine on the fish are also probably not going to be a problem for a nano pond.

Insect predators, however, are a concern. The graceful, iridescent dragonflies and darning needles that may flit over the surface of your pond feeding on mosquitoes will leave behind eggs that hatch into voracious nymphs. While we considered these animals as potential nano aquarium residents, they will prey on small fish in a nano pond. A few fish suitable for nano ponds might be able to consume the nymphs, especially when they first hatch, but if all your nano pond fish are small mouthed, you should be alert and check among the plants and bottom detritus periodically for the insects, which can be netted out.

Dragonflies will leave eggs in your nano pond that will hatch and the resulting nymphs may terrorize small fish.

Mosquitoes, of course, prey on us, and they can carry dangerous diseases. Fortunately, even the smallest fish will greedily feed on mosquito larvae, so it is very unlikely that a nano pond will become a mosquito breeding ground. If you do notice the comma-shaped larvae hanging at the surface or moving jerkily through the water, add a few more fish to deal with the population.

Specimen Display

Very often the star of a nano pond is a plant, often a water lily. A dwarf lily accompanied by three 2-inch (5-cm) celestial goldfish in a whiskey barrel would make a unique garden display, as would a single larger lionhead.

A lionhead goldfish.

Community Display

A nano pond used to house your aquarium's fish during the summer can make an attractive community display. Or you can create a community just for the pond. Most pond fish are rather large, in order to be seen from a distance, but a nano pond should invite you to kneel down and peer in. Thus you can make communities of smaller fish.

Biotope Display

Probably the most fun would be to make a display of your local biotope. Being careful to obey all regulations, you could stock your pond completely with plants and animals you collect yourself—by limiting your collection to areas of still, shallow water you will automatically select species that will fare well in a nano pond.

The Cutting Edge

Chapter **11**

Where are nano tanks heading? Besides becoming more and more popular and proliferating in form, they are branching into new areas, pushing the nano envelope as it were. Before considering some of the novel ways in which the nano concept is being applied to larger or more complex systems, let's consider two ways in which the concept is being realized in terms of novel inhabitants.

Pests or Pets?

First is the keeping of species that most aquarists consider pests—or even scourges. We've already seen some of these unusual nano specimens, such as dragonfly nymphs and *Aiptasia* anemones. The mini aquarium permits us to appreciate and enjoy the beauty and behavior of animals whose habits make them unwelcome in a regular aquarium setup. The nano focus can change them from detested to prize specimens. Let's consider a few additional possibilities.

Aiptasia sp.

Mantis Shrimp

These animals in the order Stomatopoda are supreme predators, with a horrible reputation in the aquarium hobby because of their appetite for just about any other living animal in their tank. There are many species, with the largest 8 to 16 inches (20 to 40 cm), but most are much smaller. They stow away in live rock and once established in a reef aquarium can be extremely hard to extirpate. Just about the only way to remove one is to trap it. Just make sure the trap is acrylic and not glass, since the animal can easily smash its way out of a glass container.

They are, however, extremely colorful creatures, and their unusual shape and extreme behaviors make them fascinating specimens. Depending on species, mantis shrimp (see Figure 11.1) have either a claw modified into a sledgehammer or one crafted as a barbed spear. Never subtle, a hungry mantis might pound a clam's shell to pieces or impale a fish to get a meal. The name "thumb splitter" was given to the mantis shrimp by fishermen who often suffer a maimed appendage when they inadvertently come upon one of these animals in their nets. Specimens have been known to crack thick aquarium glass with their lightning-fast attacks. The speed and force with which they strike is enormous—more than 10,000 gees—and the secondary shock wave can stun or kill the target even if the initial blow misses the mark.

Mantis shrimp have what may be the most sophisticated vision of any animal. It is superior in terms of acuity and color perception. In fact, they probably see an ultraviolet spectrum with as much range as we see in the (for us) visible spectrum. While humans see with four color pigments, stomatopods have that many just for ultraviolet discrimination, and another four just for viewing polarized light. Not impressed yet? Well, mantis shrimp are extremely long lived—20 years or more—and they demonstrate considerable intelligence. They also communicate with each other in various ways, including fluorescence, and they show complex social behaviors.

Figure 11.1

Mantis Shrimp

Odontodactylus sp.

Odontodactylus scyllarus

Squilla empusa

Acrylic Only

Mantis shrimp should be housed only in acrylic vessels. Otherwise there is the chance that their powerful claws can crack or even smash open the glass tank.

In other words, they are ideal candidates for a single-specimen setup, preferably in an acrylic vessel. It is probably possible for a mantis shrimp to crack acrylic, but it takes much more force to break than glass does, and the resultant damage is less dangerous. With a few pieces of live rock to provide cover, a mantis shrimp can make a fascinating pet. Chunks of fish or shellfish should be readily taken. Just make sure you do not ever try to handfeed your mantis. In fact, never place your hands into the aquarium unless the animal is completely fenced off with a piece of plastic.

Bristleworms

Bristleworms are annelids in the class Polychaeta. With more than 10,000 species, they exhibit a gigantic range of habitat, form, and behavior. In size they range from tiny animals that float in the plankton raft to 10-foot (3-m) giants. Many have well-developed jaws. You will find contradictory information about bristleworms in hobby literature, and much of that results from the huge variety among these animals.

Small burrowing polychaetes are prized by reef aquarists who maintain deep sandbeds full of detritivores as part of their biofiltration. These small worms keep the

Bristleworm.

sand stirred and eat detritus. They also spawn, producing gametes and larvae that serve as planktonic food for sessile invertebrates. On the other hand, large bristleworms will prey on fish and topple live rock formations as they move around the tank. It is common for a worm that arrived undetected in live rock or sand to grow to the point that the first indication of its presence is missing or maimed fish.

Also fairly common is for aquarists to discover a medium-sized worm, maybe 8 or 10 inches (about 20 cm), that has learned to come out of hiding when food is dropped into the tank. The worm quickly becomes an appreciated pet. A nano system for a mid-size polychaete? Sure!

Food or Pets?

Almost any live food that is commonly cultured could also be set up in a nano tank. A 5-gallon (20-liter) vinegar eel display would be rather boring except in very bright light to someone with superlative visual acuity, but besides the scuds we already discussed, interesting setups could be made with brine shrimp, daphnia, cyclops, and other animals usually raised as feeders.

The lowly brine shrimp in the genus *Artemia* are fascinating creatures. They move around with bilateral rows of feathery oars. They are constantly on the go, making curving sweeps through the water. Their prominent eyes are interesting features, as are the clusters of eggs the females carry on themselves. While the eggs hatch and the nauplii do best in seawater salinity, the adults prefer a slightly higher salinity. Their natural diet includes bacteria and algae, but they can be fed a wide variety of tiny-

Glassworms (left), an old standby live food, are the aquatic larvae of a fly and are normally harvested from under the ice in the winter. So they aren't really candidates for a nano system, unless it was refrigerated.

Adult brine shrimp (right).

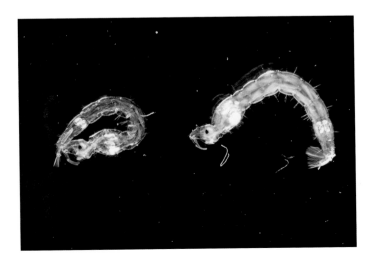

particle foods such as yeast, hardboiled egg yolk infusion, liquid fry food, and baby food vegetables. In lower salinity with plenty of food the females produce free-swimming young, but in higher salinity or when deprived of food, they produce the cysts ("eggs") that are commonly used to produce baby brine shrimp to feed to fish.

Multiple Systems

Instead of scaling equipment down to the mini aquarium, some people have scaled small displays up to equipment and created multiple systems. Freshwater aquatic gardeners and marine reefkeepers sometimes gather a row of nano tanks under a regular metal halide or other high-tech light. This, of course, results in something larger than a desktop system, but it can still be an attractive display.

Probably the first applications of centralized nano tank maintenance were the flow-through systems killie breeders created to link all of their small breeding tanks into central filtration. This was an instance of fishroom technology being scaled down for the small aquaria in which killies are bred. It took on more of a nano feel when used by betta breeders to house males in individual spaces while using regular aquarium filtration and heating to maintain them. Many of these setups were quite utilitarian, made from materials like PVC rain gutters. Simpler systems had the water pumped from and back into an aquarium with adequate heating and filtration, while other designs included tiers of flow-through compartments plumbed directly to a canister filter.

You can't keep a good idea down, and soon we saw ornamental units made of clear acrylic and designed either to hang in a regular aquarium or to be plumbed into a central heating and filtration system. This resulted in male betta displays considerably improved over the traditional row of jars; it also vastly simplified the care and maintenance of a collection of bettas, as well as vastly improving the overall health and well-being of the fish.

Fancy guppy breeders picked up on the idea and began using acrylic compartments with slotted bottoms as breeding traps for gravid females. These have all the advantages of regular breeding traps with the added significant advantage of providing a flow-through system to keep the water in each compartment as fresh as that of the aquarium in which they hang.

The Mega Nano

Since an important part of the nano concept is the focus on focusing on Nature, without an absolute size limit, there exists the possibility of having a very large aquarium that is set up with that type of focus—a big tank whose theme is zooming in on the tiny dynamics of an aquatic system.

Wall Tanks

Wall-hung aquaria were mentioned in Chapter 3. The number and design of these units are proliferating, and models are available pre-framed, with integral lighting. Designs range from hemispheric bowls that you screw to the wall to large rectangular tanks that have to be securely fastened to two or more studs. Some even have built-in speakers and MP3 technology, combining aquatic beauty with music (though it remains to be seen how fish will appreciate the vibrations magnified through their water).

The obvious limiting factor with these systems is weight. In order to be unobtrusively supported while hanging on a wall, an aquarium cannot be very heavy, and therefore not very large in volume. By keeping the tank extremely narrow (maximum 4 to 6 inches, 10 to 15 cm), a normal- size viewing panel still produces a unit that weighs less than many large paintings or filled bookshelves. The problem is that it is volume and surface area, not length, that most limit the stocking capacity of an aquarium. Both volume and surface area are quite small with these wall tanks, meaning that without the nano concept, you wind up with a few fish in a tank that looks big enough for many more—ho-hum again.

Contrast that, however, with a nano application of the same aquarium. A large number of very active nano-size fishes fill up that large viewing area without overtaxing the small volume of water behind it. We've already mentioned danios in regard to these tanks. Another great choice would be the smaller species of hatchetfish of the genus *Carnegiella*.

The Nano Focus

We can take this one step further—using standard aquaria for nano setups. When average-size fish are placed into small tanks, the result is usually unhealthy and unattractive, but when a larger aquarium is populated with nano fish, the possibilities are immense!

Dwarf cichlid breeders have observed that when they place pairs into tanks larger than the usual 5- or 10-gallon (20- or 40-liter) aquaria they usually use, the fish's behavior often changes considerably. In order to observe natural behaviors, including harem polygamy, it is necessary to give the fish sufficient

Flying Fish

If spooked or chasing food, a hatchetfish will literally take flight. Hatchetfish's powerful pectoral muscles permit them to actually fly for a couple of yards (meters) after leaping from the water. Because of this innate ability, make sure your tank's top is on tightly. (For an experimental nano setup that attempts to showcase such activity, see the "Beauty in Flight" setup later on in this chapter.)

room. Thus a nano focus might require a 6-foot (2-m) tank—tiny fish and tiny territories, but a large aggregation of them.

Another application of the nano concept that requires large tanks is the establishment of natural-looking schools of small fish. Those perennial favorites the neon tetra, *Paracheirodon innesi,* and the cardinal tetra, *Paracheirodon axelrodi,* occur naturally in schools of hundreds if not thousands of individual fish. A school of 100 such tetras requires a big aquarium—100 gallons (400 liters) or larger. But what a display! This is also the type of setup where you can feature those small-but-energetic fish like danios. The easiest way to stock a tank like this is to spawn the desired species, producing a couple of hundred fish all the same size. Tetras, barbs, danios, and rasboras can all be bred and raised for such displays.

Biotope displays are a great way to enjoy the nano focus on a mega scale. While a small desktop setup can be designed simply with aesthetics in mind, a tight focus on a larger area permits a slice of Nature to be imitated with considerable veracity. In many ways, this is what the first mini-reef aquaria were—an attempt to recreate a section of coral reef. Interestingly, it was among reef aquarists that the modern nano concept was developed as they kept focusing more and more tightly. The irony is apparent—the nano concept derived from a large reef tank can be expanded back in size to produce systems as large as or larger than the original reef setups.

A large school of *Paracheirodon axelrodi* is an awe-inspiring sight to behold.

Here now is a list of possible applications of the nano concept on a grand scale. While each would make a beautiful and fascinating display if you created it, the purpose of including them is equally to stimulate thought. As you come to embrace and appreciate this approach to aquarium keeping, you are certain to come up with many ideas of your own. Experiment and enjoy!

A North American Swamp Close-Up

Native plants and fish are increasingly available in the trade, but this can also be a tank stocked by collecting—check into and follow all local regulations. This vegetation-heavy setup will allow you to observe the life in a swamp—without the mud, muck, and smell!

This tank has no filter, so although it is lightly stocked and heavily planted, you should change 50 percent or more of the water every week.

Setup:	Livestock:
33-gallon (130-liter) long tank, 48 by 12 by 12 inches (120 by 30 by 30 cm)	Heavily planted with native species, including with emergent plants and some duckweed
Sand substrate or, better, a special plant substrate	3 small tadpoles
Driftwood and rocks for natural hiding places	6 dwarf crayfish *Cambarus schufeldtii*
Water depth of only about 6 inches (15 cm)	8 to 10 pygmy sunfish, *Elassoma* sp.
Double fluorescent fixture providing 80 watts of light	Optional: a colony of scuds

An Amazon Stream
Close-up

The tetras serve as dithers to coax the cichlids out of hiding, while the busy catfish supply the scene with energy. You can almost imagine a rivulet through the thick rainforest.

Setup:	Livestock:
40-gallon (160-liter) long tank, 48 by 13 by 16 inches (120 by 30 by 40 cm)	Two pairs of Apistogramma cichlids
Leaf litter substrate	A dozen dwarf *Corydoras* catfish
Driftwood to imitate tree roots	Two dozen small tetras of a single species, or a dozen of each of two species
A power filter or powerhead producing a current the length of the tank	
Dim lighting	

Apistogramma gibbiceps

A school of *Corydoras pygmaeus* will do well in the "Amazon Stream Close-up" setup.

A 3-Tier Amazon Stream

With about 100 fish, this tank will be extremely busy. You will be able to observe the schooling behaviors as well as individual behaviors in this close-up view of Amazonia.

Setup:	Livestock:
6-foot (2-m) tank—100, 125 gallons (400 to 500 liters), etc.	A variety of Amazon swords, *Echinodorus* spp., planted along the back, leaving the foreground open
Fine gravel substrate	Two dozen marble hatchetfish, *Carnegiella strigata* (top tier)
Driftwood	50 cardinal tetras, *Paracheirodon axelrodi* (middle tier)
2 large hang-on filters or a canister filter	Two dozen *Corydoras* catfish of a single species (bottom tier)

Echinodorus cordifolius

Carnegiella strigata

Echinodorus grisebachii

Corydoras habrosus

An Asian Stream

This is a biotope setup that concentrates on some of Asia's smaller fish in groups large enough to display natural behaviors.

Setup:	Livestock:
33-gallon (130-liter) long tank, 48 by 12 by 12 inches (120 by 30 by 30 cm)	A heavy planting of *Cryptocoryne* along the back, leaving the foreground open
Fine gravel substrate	Floating water sprite plants
Driftwood, perhaps planted with Java fern or Java moss	6 loaches of one species chosen from: 　　Yo-yo loach, *Botia almorhae* 　　Batik loach, *Botia kubotai* 　　Zebra loach, *Botia striata* 　　Any species in the genus *Yasuhikotakia*
Single or double fluorescent lighting, 40 or 80 watts	10 of one species of danio
A power filter or powerhead producing a current the length of the tank	10 *Trigonostigma heteromorpha* rasboras
	One pair of honey dwarf gouramis, *Trichogaster chuna*, or sparkling gourami, *Trichopsis pumila*

Yasuhikotakia nigrolineata, the black-lined loach.

Botia almorhae

Botia striata

Yasuhikotakia morleti,
the skunk loach.

Botia kubotai (large) with
Yasuhikotakia sidthimunki (small).

Cryptocoryne lucens

Beauty in Flight

This one is experimental. Readers should let us know if they try it and it works. What is "it"? Trying to observe these fish flying in captivity. Many animals known as "flying" are merely gliders, such as flying squirrels (subfamily Pteromyinae) and flying fish (family Exocoetidae). The hatchetfish of the family Gasteropelecidae, however, are capable of powered flight—though admittedly extremely limited powered flight. They are observed to rise as a school to feed on insects. This setup would be supplied with *Drosophila*—fruit flies that would be contained by the tight lid and that would hopefully lure the fish into the air. If it doesn't work, or if you get tired of rearing fruit flies for them, you can fill the tank and switch to any floating foods, as the fish will only eat from the surface.

Setup:	Livestock:
6-foot (2-m) tank—or longer, only half full of water	Perhaps a few *Echinodorus swords*, if lighting is sufficient, but no plants needed.
An extremely tight-fitting lid.	
Driftwood	75 marble hatchetfish, *Carnegiella strigata*, or 40 to 50 larger hatchetfish such as *Thoracocharax* spp. or *Gasteropelecus* spp.
A canister filter with input and output tubes at opposite ends of the tank	

Thoracocharax stellatus

Gasteropelecus sp.

The Sky's the Limit!

The possibilities are truly endless. Applying the nano microscope to the biotope can focus on the microhabitat among a mangrove tree's roots. This could be replicated fairly well on the nano level with a few gallons of brackish water, a few invertebrates, and a killie or two. Or it could be realized in a vivarium 8 feet tall and 6 feet wide (2$\frac{1}{2}$ meters tall and 2 meters wide), with an actual stand of live mangroves, crustaceans, mudskippers, and other fish. It could have a sump/reservoir and a couple of pumps and switches to cause the "tide" to rise and fall throughout the day.

A nano focus on a single species could be a half dozen cardinal tetras, *Paracheirodon axelrodi,* in a 5-gallon (20-liter) desktop or in a 1,000-gallon (3,800-liter) aquarium with a school of 1,000 tetras.

The next time you contemplate a new aquarium setup, keep the nano concept in mind. And if you are planning a desktop tank, especially keep it in mind so that instead of a crowded "ho-hum" you can create a beautiful and meaningful "wow!"

Resources

Magazine
Tropical Fish Hobbyist
1 TFH Plaza
3rd & Union Avenues
Neptune City, NJ 07753
E-mail: info@tfh.com
www.tfhmagazine.com

Internet Resources
Aquaria Central
www.aquariacentral.com

Aquarium Hobbyist
www.aquariumhobbyist.com

Cichlid Forum
www.cichlid-forum.com

FishBase
www.fishbase.org

Fish Geeks
www.fishgeeks.com

Gobioid Research Institute
http://gobiidae.com

Loaches Online
www.loaches.com

Marine Aquarium Advice
www.marineaquariumadvice.com

Planet Catfish
www.planetcatfish.com

Reef Central
www.reefcentral.com

Tropical Resources
www.tropicalresources.net

Wet Web Media
www.wetwebmedia.com

A World of Fish
www.aworldoffish.com

Associations and Societies
American Cichlid Association
E-mail: IvyRose@optonline.net
www.cichlid.org

American Killifish Association
www.aka.org

American Livebearers Association
http://livebearers.org

Federation of American Aquarium Societies (FAAS)
E-mail: Jbenes01@yahoo.com
www.faas.info

Marine Aquarium Council (MAC)
E-mail: info@aquariumcouncil.org
www.aquariumcouncil.org

Marine Aquarium Societies of North America (MASNA)
E-mail: secretary@masna.org
www.masna.org

Books

Barber, Terry Anne. *Setup and Care of Garden Ponds.*
TFH Publications, Inc.

Barber, Terry Anne. *The Simple Guide to Garden Ponds.*
TFH Publications, Inc.

Barber, Terry Anne and Rhonda Wilson.
The Simple Guide to Planted Aquariums.
TFH Publications, Inc.

Boruchowitz, David E. *Aquarium Care of Bettas.*
TFH Publications, Inc.

Boruchowitz, David E. *Setup and Care of
Saltwater Aquariums.*
TFH Publications, Inc.

Boruchowitz, David E. *The Simple Guide to
Freshwater Aquariums.*
TFH Publications, Inc.

Brightwell, CR. *Marine Chemistry.*
TFH Publications, Inc.

Brightwell, Chris R. *The Nano-Reef Handbook.*
TFH Publications, Inc.

Dickinson, Claudia. *Aquarium Care of Cichlids.*
TFH Publications, Inc.

Edmonds, Devin. *Tree Frogs.*
TFH Publications, Inc.

Fatherree, James W. *The Super Simple Guide to Corals.*
TFH Publications, Inc.

Fenner, Robert F. *The Conscientious Marine Aquarist.*
Microcosm/TFH Publications, Inc.

Hemdal, Jay F. *Advanced Marine Aquarium Techniques.*
TFH Publications, Inc.

Kurtz, Jeffrey. *The Simple Guide to Marine Aquariums.*
TFH Publications, Inc.

Kurtz, Jeffrey. *The Simple Guide to
Mini-Reef Aquariums.*
TFH Publications, Inc.

Macdonald, Mark and Martin Thoene, eds. *Loaches.*
TFH Publications, Inc.

Michael, Scott W. *Adventurous Aquarist Guide™: The
101 Best Saltwater Fishes.*
Microcosm/TFH Publications, Inc.

Michael, Scott W. *A PocketExpert™ Guide to
Marine Fishes.*
Microcosm/TFH Publications, Inc.

Michael, Scott W. *A PocketExpert™ Guide to
Reef Aquarium Fishes.*
Microcosm/TFH Publications, Inc.

Monks, Neale, ed. *Brackish-Water Fishes.*
TFH Publications, Inc.

Purser, Philip. *Natural Terrariums.*
TFH Publications, Inc.

Shimek, Ronald L. *A PocketExpert™ Guide to
Marine Invertebrates.*
Microcosm/TFH Publications, Inc.

Shubel, Stan. *Aquarium Care of Fancy Guppies.*
TFH Publications, Inc.

Sihler, Amanda and Greg. *Poison Dart Frogs.*
TFH Publications, Inc.

Ward, Ashley. *Questions & Answers on
Freshwater Aquarium Fishes.*
TFH Publications, Inc.

Ward, Ashley. *Questions & Answers on Saltwater
Aquarium Fishes.*
TFH Publications, Inc.

Wilkerson, Joyce D. *Clownfishes.*
Microcosm/TFH Publications, Inc.

Wittenrich, Matthew L. *The Complete Illustrated
Breeder's Guide to Marine Aquarium Fishes.*
Microcosm/TFH Publications, Inc.

Wood, Kathleen. *Adventurous Aquarist Guide™:
The 101 Best Tropical Fishes.*
Microcosm/TFH Publications, Inc.

Note: **Boldfaced** numbers indicate illustrations; *t* indicates a table.

Ecsenius spp., 159–160, 159
   E. bandanus, 160
   E. bicolor (Bicolor blenny), 159, **159**
   E. gravieri (Mimic blenny), 159
   E. midas (Midas blenny), 160, **160**
   E. trilineatus, 160

Photo Credits

Abbreviations: C= Column, R= Row, T= Top, M= Middle, B=Bottom, L= Left, RI= Right. For columns and rows: C1, R2, etc.= Column 1, Row 2, etc. Please note that some of the abbreviations have been combined: MT= Middle Top, TRI= Top Right, C1B= Column 1 Bottom, R1RI= Row 1 Right, etc.

Joe Aliperti: 104, 110

Bob Allen: 93 (R1), 125 (B)

GR Allen: 181 (BL)

Charles Arneson: 150 (C1B)

John Austin (Shutterstock): 240

Laurence Azoulay: 50, 92 (C1T, C1M)

Randall D. Babb: 192 (C2T), 201 (C3M)

Marian Bacon: 200 (R1, R2RI, R3M), 201 (C3B)

RD Bartlett: 102 (C1T), 129, 192 (C3T), 200 (R2M)

Marius Burger: 201 (C2M, C2B)

Angel Cánovas: 62 (C1M, C1B, C2T, C3T), 70 (C1MT, C1B), 72 (C1B), 73 (C1T, C3T, C3MB), 117, 125 (T)

Kok Hang Choo: 227 (C1T)

Ronald Coleman: 11

G. Dibley: 220 (L)

Anna Dzondzua (Shutterstock): 19

Edgewater Media (Shutterstock): 48

Devin Edmonds: 194, 205

Graeme Edwards: 107

James Fatherree: 168 (T), 181 (BRI), 228, 255

Robert M. Fenner: 144 (R1RI), 154 (L)

Greg Fiske: 106

Andy Foden: 99

Alex Franklin: 203 (C1MB)

Paul Freed: 191 (B), 192 (C2B, C3B), 200 (C1T, C1B), 203 (C1B)

U. Erich Friese: 227 (C1B)

Bill Gately: 73 (C2B), 140

James E. Gerholdt: 200 (R3RI)

Michael Gilroy: 73 (C3MT), 121, 223, 229 (L)

Joe Goodson (Shutterstock): 221

Jess Gracia: 175

Harry Grier: 97 (R2RI, R3M)

Jay F. Hemdal: 15, 150 (C3M), 203 (C1MT), 207

Joanne Hueter: 158

Ray Hunziker: 119, 203 (C1T)

Johnny Jensen: 62 (C3M), 63 (R1L, R1M, R1RI, R2L, R3M), 160 (T), 161 (C1B), 162 (B), 165 (R1M), 166 (B), 206

Wendy Kaveney Photography (Shutterstock): 27

Ng Wei Keong (Shutterstock): 8

Karl Knaack: 72 (C1MB), 78 (BRI), 162 (T), 245

S. Kornobis: 109

Gary Lange: 68, 131, 144 (R2L, R3RI), 179 (L)

Michael Ledray (Shutterstock): 24

James Lee: 57, 186, 208

Horst Linke: 216

Gillian Lisle: 220

Erik Loza: 201 (C2T)

Oliver Lucanus: 17, 30 (R1RI, R2RI, R3RI), 62 (C3B), 65 (B), 72 (C1T), 75 (C1MB), 78 (BL), 79 (TM, BRI), 85 (C3M, C3B), 86 (C2B, C3M), 87 (C1B, C2T, C3T), 89 (RI), 93 (R2RI, R3L), 96 (C2M, C2B, C3T, C3M), 97 (R3L), 162 (BL)

Ken Lucas: 156

H. Mayer: 116 (C1B)

John Mehe: 94

G. & C. Merker: 130, 132

Michael Metheny (Shutterstock): 169

Dmitrijs Mihejevs (Shutterstock): 114, 241 (M)

Aaron Norman: 25, 28, 69 (B), 73 (C1B), 84, 96 (C1B), 101 (C1T), 102 (C1B), 118 (L), 120 (C1B), 123 (BRI), 150 (C3B), 199, 232

John O'Malley: 93 (R3RI), 126 (C1B), 134, 150 (C1M), 179 (RI), 184 (C1T)

Alvaro Pantoja (Shutterstock): 188

Klaus Paysan: 6

MP. & C. Piednoir: 4, 22, 31, 34, 49 (R1MT, R1MB), 52, 63 (R3L, R3RI), 66 (T), 69 (TL, TRI), 70 (C1MB), 71 (RI), 74, 85 (C2B), 87 (C3B), 93 (R2M), 115, 120 (C1T), 123 (T), 128, 161 (C1MB), 165 (R1RI), 180 (C1MB), 181 (T), 184 (C1B), 196 (C1T, C1MT, C1MB), 211, 235 (TL, BL), 238

Courtney Platt: 150 (C2T)

Proaquatix: 182

Philip Purser: 195

Sasha Radosavljevich (Shutterstock): 35

Curtis Ramsey: 237 (R3L)

J. Randall: 151

Styve Reineck (Shutterstock): 172

Hans-Joachim Richter: 62 (C2B), 73 (C1MB, C2T), 76, 88 (TL), 97 (R2M), 234 (L)

Fred Rohde: 83 (T)

Fred Rosenzweig: 222

Andre Roth: 73 (C2MT), 88 (BM, BRI)

Lisa Saad Photography (Shutterstock): 12

JJ Scheel: 96 (C2T)

G. Schmelzer: 93 (R2L), 180 (C1MT)

Dr. Jürgen Schmidt: 85 (C1T, C1M, C2T), 86 (C1T, C3T), 87 (C1T, C3M)

Craig Sernotti: 45

Dr. Dwight Smith: 143

Mark Smith: 38, 65 (T), 70 (C1T), 71 (L), 80 (B), 96 (R1, R2L, R3RI), 103 (T), 111, 118 (RI), 120 (C1M), 144 (R1L, R1M, R2RI, R3L, R3M), 145, 146 (C1T, C1B), 147, 149, 150 (C1T), 153, 154 (RI), 155 (C1M, C1B), 157, 159, 160 (BRI), 161 (C1MT), 165 (R1L, R2M, R2RI, R3), 168 (B), 187 (T), 192 (C1B, C2M), 201 (C1M), 214 (B), 227 (C1M)

W. Sommer: 30 (R2L), 73 (C1MT)

Marc S. Staniszewski: 101 (C1B), 200 (R2L)

Walter A. Stark II: 141

Rony Suzuki: 239

Karl H. Switak: 200 (R3L), 201 (C3T)

Zoltan Takacs: 123 (BL)

Kenjiro Tanaka: 86 (C1B), 87 (C1M, C2B), 91 (R2L), 96 (C3B)

Iggy Tavares: 92 (C1B), 166 (T), 168 (M), 170, 235 (TRI), 242

Ed Taylor: 5 (RI), 30 (R1L), 49 (R1T), 83 (B), 86 (C3B), 108, 126 (C1M), 196 (C1B), 197 (C1T, C1B), 237 (R2/R3RI)

Emma Turner: 236

Marc Turner: 103 (B)

Anthony Vastano: 78 (T), 142, 187 (B), 241 (RI)

Nicholas Violand: 32, 39

Damien Wagaman: 58, 112

Maleta M. Walls: 229 (RI)

Weiyee (Shutterstock): 215

Rhonda Wilson: 126 (C1T)

Matthew L. Wittenrich: 180 (C1B)

Lein de León Yong (Shutterstock): 212

Fábio Augusto Yoshida: Cover/Title Page, 224

Dr. Karel Zahrádka: 89 (L)

Joanna Zopoth-Lipiejko (Shutterstock): 204 (BL, BRI)

R. Zukal: 75 (C1T)

All other photos courtesy of the TFH Photo Archives